the BIBLE story

Onward to Glory

(From the Ascension to His Coming Kingdom)

VOLUME TEN

the Bible Story

Onward to Glory ❖ Volume Ten

Arthur S. Maxwell
Author of Uncle Arthur's *Bedtime Stories*

When Arthur S. Maxwell wrote *The Bible Story*, he used the King James Version of the Bible, closely following its narrative. This edition continues that tradition and draws from other translations using language that today's children readily understand.

NEWLY REVISED AND ILLUSTRATED

More than 400 stories in 10 Volumes Covering the Entire Bible From Genesis to Revelation

REVIEW AND HERALD® PUBLISHING ASSOCIATION
HAGERSTOWN, MD 21740

Illustrations not individually
credited are by C. d'Andrea, F.
Collins, S. Dunlap, W.
Heaslip, W. Hutchinson, M.
Lee, D. Loomis, T. K. Martin,
V. Nye, L. Quade, P. Remmey,
and H. Rudeen..

Unless otherwise noted, all
Bible verses are from the *Holy
Bible, New International Version.*
Copyright © 1973, 1978, 1983,
International Bible Society.
Used by permission of
Zondervan Bible Publishers.
Bible texts credited to TEV are
from the *Good News Bible—*
Old Testament: Copyright ©
American Bible Society 1976;
New Testament: Copyright ©
American Bible Society 1966,
1971, 1976. Bible texts credited
to NRSV are from the New
Revised Standard Version
Bible, copyright © 1989,
Division of Christian
Education of the National
Council of Churches of Christ
in the U.S.A.

This book was
Revised by Cheryl Holloway
Edited by Eugene Lincoln
Cover art by Harry Anderson

PRINTED IN U.S.A.

R&H Cataloging Service
Maxwell, Arthur Stanley,
1896-1970
     The Bible story.
     1. Bible stories.   I. Title.
II. Holloway, Cheryl Woolsey,
1956-
          220.9505

ISBN 0-8280-0804-3

**As the astonished
disciples saw Jesus
ascend into heaven, an
angel cried, "Why stand
ye gazing up into heaven?
this same Jesus . . . shall
so come . . . as ye have
seen him go."**

PAINTING BY RUSSELL HARLAN

C O N T E N T S

PART THREE—Stories of the First Christian Letters

PART FOUR—Stories of Christ's Final Triumph

Indexes

PART ONE

Stories of

the First
Christian
Church

(Acts 1:12-12:19)

The Flame From Heaven

(Acts 1:12-15; 2:1-4)

HOW HAPPY the angels must have been on that glorious ascension day! I can almost feel their radiant gladness, can't you? Joyfully they crowd around their beloved Lord as they speed heavenward singing David's victory song:

"Lift up your heads, O you gates;
be lifted up, you ancient doors,
that the King of glory may come in."

"Who is this King of glory?" asks a voice from the dwelling place of God.

The angels sing triumphantly,
"The Lord strong and mighty,
the Lord mighty in battle.
Lift up your heads, O you gates;
lift them up, you ancient doors,
that the King of glory may come in." [1]

Jesus is the great Conqueror. He has battled with Satan and won. He has died and risen again. He has proved that God's

9

After His life of toil and sacrifice Jesus ascended to heaven where He was joyfully received by the angelic hosts, many of whom had attended Him in His last sufferings.

love is stronger than the devil's hate, and that all of Satan's plans must fail.

Now He takes the place waiting for Him "at the right hand of the Majesty in heaven." [2] But does He, in the middle of all this glory, forget His humble followers on the earth? No indeed. Instead He watches over them more lovingly than ever, hoping they will not fail Him.

He talks with the angels about them—about Peter, James, John, Thomas, and all the rest—so that they too become deeply interested in His earthly friends. Eagerly they wait for His call to fly to their help when they are in trouble.

Meanwhile, down on the earth, there is excitement in a certain room in Jerusalem. It is packed to the doors with 120 people. Among them are the 11 disciples, who have just seen Jesus go up to heaven from the top of the Mount of Olives. The others are full of questions.

"Did you really see Him go up into the sky?" asks one. "How far did He go before you couldn't see Him anymore?"

"And about that cloud," asks another. "Was it a real cloud or a cloud of angels?"

"Tell us about the two young men in white," urges some-body else. "Are you sure Jesus sent them? Did they really say Jesus would come back someday?"

They remember how He told them to wait in Jerusalem until they received "power from on high." What can this mean? What power? What for? What will it do to them?

Nobody can answer these questions. They will have to wait and see. But they feel that if Jesus is going to send them power from heaven, they must get ready to receive it. So they begin to pray, and continue in prayer.

They have some wonderful prayer meetings. I can hear them thanking God for sending Jesus from heaven to live with them and die for them. I can hear them, too, thanking Him for the friendship of Jesus and for all the lovely times they had together with Him.

And I am sure some of them tell God how much they need courage and strength to witness for Jesus, and how they want to be brave and good and true.

As they come closer to God they draw closer to one another. Some begin to ask forgiveness for hasty words they have said or for unkind deeds they have done. There are tears in many eyes as some clasp hands, saying, "Of course I forgive you. Please forgive me!" So they all begin to know something of the joy that comes from keeping that beautiful commandment of Jesus: "Love each other as I have loved you."

Day after day they stay together, waiting for Jesus to keep His promise, waiting for the power from heaven. Then, just seven weeks after the crucifixion, on the day of Pentecost, something very wonderful happens.

Suddenly there is "a sound like the blowing of a violent

wind." It rattles the windows, slams the doors, shakes the whole house.

Then a tongue of fire appears on every one of them. Those at the back of the room see these tongues flaming over Peter, James, John, and the rest of the apostles, while they, in turn, see them flashing from the humblest disciples present.

For a moment it seems as though the whole house is on fire. And in a way it is!

Until this moment the room has been hushed and quiet. Only the voices of people praying have been heard. Now, this rushing wind and these tongues of flame have changed them all. In one swift moment everybody is filled with zeal and activity. They feel they have prayed enough; now they must go out and tell the world about their risen Lord.

From this fire-filled room 120 men and women go out, on fire for God, eager to carry the light of His love to every part of the earth.

[1] Psalm 24:7-9.
[2] Hebrews 1:3.
[3] Luke 24:49.
[4] John 15:12.

Men on Fire

(Acts 2:5-42)

AS THE disciples spread through Jerusalem, on fire with the good news about Jesus, they experience a big surprise. All the foreign visitors in Jerusalem seem to understand what they are saying!

The faces of strangers from other lands light up as they hear the message of the love of Jesus from these humble, uneducated men. "Are not all these men who are speaking Galileans?" they ask, "Then how is it that each of us hears them in his own native language?"

It is beyond belief that these men from northern Palestine, who have never been to school, can talk to "Parthians, Medes and Elamites; residents of Mesopotamia, Judea and Cappadocia, Pontus and Asia; Phrygia and Pamphylia, Egypt and the parts of Libya near Cyrene; visitors from Rome; . . . Cretans and Arabs."

"How can it be," ask these foreigners, "that we hear them declaring the wonders of God in our own tongues!"

"They must be drunk," says someone. "They have had too much wine."

This is too much for Peter. He knows the true answer. The King of glory has remembered His old friends and has sent them the promised power.

Standing where he can be seen and heard, he cries, "Fellow Jews and all of you who live in Jerusalem. . . . These men are not drunk, as you suppose. It's only nine in the morning! No, this is what was spoken by the prophet Joel: 'In the last days, God says, I will pour out my Spirit on all people. Your sons and daughters will prophesy, your young men will see visions, your old men will dream dreams. . . .

"Men of Israel, listen to this: Jesus of Nazareth was a man accredited by God to you by miracles, wonders and signs, which God did among you through him, as you yourselves know. . . .

"You, with the help of wicked men, put him to death by nailing him to the cross. But God raised him from the dead, freeing him from the agony of death, because it was impossible for death to keep its hold on him. . . .

"Brothers, I can tell you confidently that the patriarch David died and was buried, and his tomb is here to this day. But he was a prophet. . . . He spoke of the resurrection of the Christ. . . .

"God has raised this Jesus to life, and we are all witnesses of the fact. Exalted to the right hand of God, he has received from the Father the promised Holy Spirit and has poured out what you now see and hear."

What a sermon! With flashing eyes and powerful voice, Peter tells about Jesus—His life, His death, His resurrection, and the wonderful way He fulfilled the ancient prophecies.

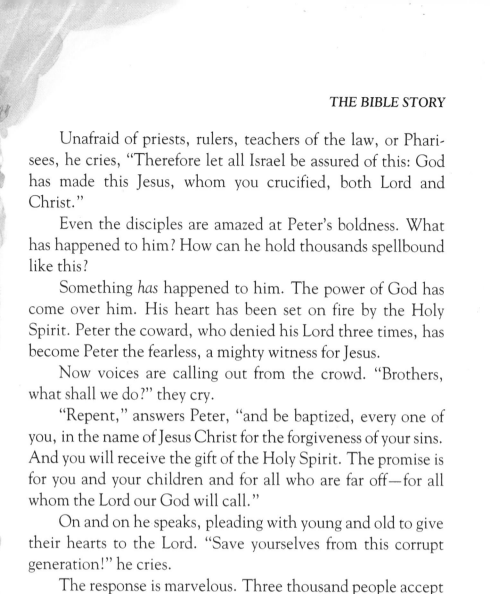

Unafraid of priests, rulers, teachers of the law, or Pharisees, he cries, "Therefore let all Israel be assured of this: God has made this Jesus, whom you crucified, both Lord and Christ."

Even the disciples are amazed at Peter's boldness. What has happened to him? How can he hold thousands spellbound like this?

Something *has* happened to him. The power of God has come over him. His heart has been set on fire by the Holy Spirit. Peter the coward, who denied his Lord three times, has become Peter the fearless, a mighty witness for Jesus.

Now voices are calling out from the crowd. "Brothers, what shall we do?" they cry.

"Repent," answers Peter, "and be baptized, every one of you, in the name of Jesus Christ for the forgiveness of your sins. And you will receive the gift of the Holy Spirit. The promise is for you and your children and for all who are far off—for all whom the Lord our God will call."

On and on he speaks, pleading with young and old to give their hearts to the Lord. "Save yourselves from this corrupt generation!" he cries.

The response is marvelous. Three thousand people accept Jesus—and the Christian church is born.

A Beggar Healed

(Acts 3:1-4:4)

WHEN the fire of God came into their hearts, the disciples discovered that they could not only preach but heal! Besides being able to talk in several languages, they could make people well from all sorts of diseases. They had become both preachers and doctors.

Instead of one person performing miracles, there were more than 100. The work that Jesus did alone was now done by many. No wonder all Jerusalem was stirred!

Going up to the Temple one day, Peter and John saw a lame man being carried by his friends to the gate where he sat each day asking passersby for money.

They had seen him there many times before and had felt sorry for him. Now they could really help him. "Look at us!" said Peter, to call the lame man's attention.

The beggar looked, expecting a gift, but the apostles had something far better for him than money. "Silver or gold I do not have," said Peter, "but what I have I give you. In the name of Jesus Christ of Nazareth, walk."

Taking the lame man by the hand, Peter raised him up. Immediately his feet and ankles became strong. "He jumped to his feet and began to walk. Then he went with them into the temple courts, walking and jumping, and praising God."

You can imagine what happened next. As the healed man clung to Peter and John in joy and gratitude, "all the people were astonished and came running to them." Pushing and shoving, the crowd pressed forward to see this great sight.

Everybody knew this poor man. They had seen him begging at the Temple gate for years—ever since he was a boy. He had been lame for more than 40 years. Yet here he was walking and leaping about in the most amazing way. What a miracle!

As the people crowded around, Peter saw another opportunity to tell them about Jesus. "Men of Israel," he cried in a voice that could be heard above the hubbub, "why does this surprise you? Why do you stare at us as if by our own power or godliness we had made this man walk?"

Then he went on to tell how it was really Jesus who had done it. "By faith in the name of Jesus, this man whom you see and know was made strong. It is Jesus' name and the faith that comes through him that has given this complete healing to him, as you can all see."

Then Peter pleaded with the people to repent of their sins and give their hearts to Jesus. As he spoke more and more people joined the crowd, until almost everybody in the Temple was there.

Many of the priests came to listen too, and they were anything but pleased—especially when they heard Peter say,

19

← PAINTING BY RUSSELL HARLAN

Outside the Beautiful Gate of the Temple a poor beggar who had been lame all his life was healed by Peter, who said, "In the name of Jesus Christ of Nazareth rise up and walk."

"You disowned the Holy and Righteous One and asked that a murderer be released to you. You killed the author of life, but God raised him from the dead."

This was the very thing the priests were afraid of! The disciples of Jesus were claiming that their leader had been raised from the dead! This must be stopped at once. They called the Temple guard, but Peter went on unafraid.

With deep tenderness he said, "Now, brothers, I know that you acted in ignorance, as did your leaders. But this is how God fulfilled what he had foretold through all the prophets, saying that his Christ would suffer. Repent, then, and turn to God, so that your sins may be wiped out, that times of refreshing may come from the Lord, and that he may send the Christ, who has been appointed for you—even Jesus. He must remain in heaven until the time comes for God to restore everything, as he promised long ago through his holy prophets. . . .

"And you are heirs of the prophets and of the covenant God made with your fathers. He said to Abraham, 'Through your offspring all peoples on earth will be blessed.' When God raised up his servant, he sent him first to you to bless you by turning each of you from your wicked ways."

At this moment the captain of the Temple guard forced his way through the crowd and arrested both Peter and John and led them away to prison. But he was too late. The people had heard the message. As they went to their homes that night many more decided that Jesus of Nazareth was the Christ, the Saviour of the world.

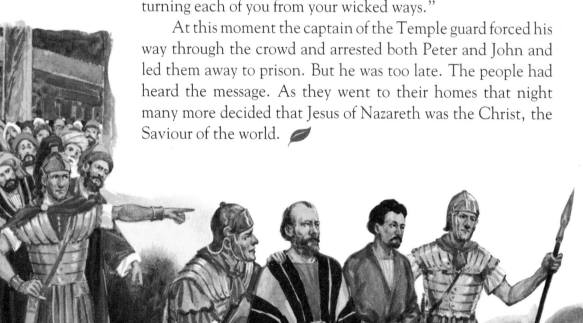

From Prisoners to Preachers

(Acts 4:5-31; 5:12-42)

THE NEXT morning the Temple leaders met together. Annas and Caiaphas, the very ones who had presided at the trial of Jesus, were there. Peter and John were called before them.

"By what power or what name did you do this?" asked the high priest.

Without a trace of fear Peter replied, "It is by the name of Jesus Christ of Nazareth, whom you crucified but whom God raised from the dead, that this man stands before you healed."

"Salvation is found in no one else," he added, "for there is no other name under heaven given to men by which we must be saved."

Peter told his story again, speaking so boldly that the priests and rulers were astonished. They couldn't understand how a poor, uneducated fisherman could talk like this. As for the miracle that had happened, they couldn't say a thing. Not only was the man who had been healed known to every one of them, but he was standing beside the two apostles, ready to

21

speak up for them if necessary.

"What are we going to do with these men?" the priests asked each other when the council room had been cleared. "Everybody living in Jerusalem knows they have done an outstanding miracle, and we cannot deny it."

Finally they decided that they would tell the apostles that they must not preach about Jesus anymore and then let them go. But they did not realize the kind of men these fishermen had become.

When they were called back into court and informed of the decision of the priests and rulers, "Peter and John replied, 'Judge for yourselves whether it is right in God's sight to obey you rather than God. For we cannot help speaking about what we have seen and heard.' "

"You had better not!" said the high priest. But the apostles went away with no thought of stopping their work. Later, in their upper room, they had a wonderful time together, thanking God for the way He had helped them and praying for strength to witness even more boldly in the future.

"Now, Lord," prayed one of them, "consider their threats and enable your servants to speak your word with great bold-

22

ness. Stretch out your hand to heal and perform miraculous signs and wonders through the name of your holy servant Jesus."

The prayer was answered. More power came from heaven. More people were healed. More great sermons were preached. "With great power the apostles continued to testify to the resurrection of the Lord Jesus, and much grace was upon them all."

"The apostles performed many miraculous signs and wonders among the people. . . . As a result, people brought the sick into the streets and laid them on beds and mats so that at least Peter's shadow might fall on some of them as he passed by."

It was just like the days when Jesus had been there! People began flocking into Jerusalem from nearby villages, "bringing their sick and those tormented by evil spirits, and all of them were healed."

This was too much for the priests and rulers. They became very angry. They could not bear to see these followers of Jesus more popular than themselves. So once more they had them arrested and put in prison.

But these men couldn't be imprisoned. No sooner were they in than they were out again.

"During the night an angel of the Lord opened the doors of

the jail and brought them out. 'Go, stand in the temple courts,' he said, 'and tell the people the full message of this new life.' "

So Peter and John went straight from the prison back to preaching once again. There in the Temple, they went on witnessing for Jesus just as though nothing had happened.

The best part of the story is that the priests knew nothing about the apostles' escape. They got ready for their trial and "sent to the jail for the apostles." But they weren't there. In a great fluster the officers returned, saying, "We found the jail securely locked, with the guards standing at the doors; but when we opened them, we found no one inside."

You can imagine the feelings of everyone in that council room. "What!" everyone cried. "The prisoners gone? Where can they be? How did they escape through locked doors?"

Suddenly a messenger came rushing in with the astounding news that the escaped prisoners were actually "standing in the temple courts teaching the people."

24

"Bring them here!" cried the chief priest, and the guard went after them. They were soon back with Peter and several others.

"We gave you strict orders not to teach in this name," said the high priest hotly. "Yet you have filled Jerusalem with your teaching and are determined to make us guilty of this man's blood."

"We must obey God rather than men!" said Peter, which made the priests and rulers more angry still.

Just then Gamaliel stood up. He was a member of the council and "was honored by all the people."

"Consider carefully what you intend to do to these men . . . ," he warned. "For if their purpose or activity is of human origin, it will fail. But if it is from God, you will not be able to stop these men."

Gamaliel's words were wise ones, and the council listened to them. It was decided to let the apostles off with a beating.

The lashes hurt, but when the beating was over, "the apostles left the Sanhedrin, rejoicing because they had been counted worthy of suffering disgrace for the Name. Day after day, in the temple courts and from house to house, they never stopped teaching and proclaiming the good news that Jesus is the Christ."

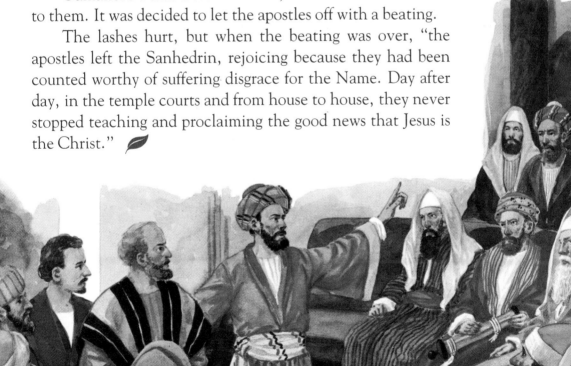

Sons of Encouragement

(Acts 4:32-5:11)

I T SEEMS hard to believe, but within a few months of the crucifixion of Jesus 5,000 people had accepted Him as their Saviour and been baptized in His name. These men, women, and their families must have been quite a sizable part of the population of Jerusalem at that time. No wonder the priests and rulers were upset!

The new believers were full of love for their Lord and for one another. The Bible says that they "were one in heart and mind. No one claimed that any of his possessions was his own, but they shared everything they had. . . . There were no needy persons among them. For from time to time those who owned lands or houses sold them, brought the money from the sales and put it at the apostles' feet, and it was distributed to anyone as he had need."

One of those who sold a field and brought the money to the apostles was a man called Joseph, a native of Cyprus. He gave his gift so gladly, so graciously, that everybody was cheered. Peter, John, and the others were so happy about it that they

26

gave him the nickname Barnabas, which means "Son of Encouragement."

What a lovely name! Wouldn't you like somebody to call you that someday? Maybe Mother or Dad? Do you know how to make this happen? Just try being like Joseph from Cyprus. Do all you are asked to do with a happy, cheerful spirit.

Sons and daughters of encouragement are welcome everywhere. They are wanted at home, at school, and in church. Parents, teachers, preachers, and businessmen are always looking for them.

Not all the people, however, were so nice about helping the early church as Barnabas was. Some brought their money grudgingly. Some thought the apostles were asking too much. Others said this pooling of the money wasn't a good idea at all.

Among these were a man named Ananias and his wife Sapphira. They had heard the message about the wonderful Teacher of Nazareth who had risen from the dead. They loved His teachings and believed He must be the Messiah of Israel.

And when they saw many of the new disciples selling their property and giving the money to the apostles to feed the poor and help the work, they felt that they should do the same.

So they dedicated a piece of land to God and sold it. The Bible doesn't say how much money they received, but it was probably quite a large amount, and more than they had expected.

When the money was in their hands, they counted it several times. Soon they began to feel that it was really too much to give just then. Maybe they should keep some for themselves. After all, there was that comfortable couch Ananias would like to have and that beautiful new dress Sapphira wanted so much.

They talked it over together and decided to give a part—a nice, large part—to God and keep the rest. Who would know that they weren't giving all they had promised? And couldn't they do what they liked with their own money?

Putting the coins in a bag, Ananias set out for the place where Peter was receiving the people's gifts. He felt sure that the apostle would praise him warmly for giving so much.

But when he got there, he found he couldn't look Peter in

the eye. He felt a strong urge to put the moneybag on the table and run. Something bothered him. Peter seemed to be looking clear through him, reading his thoughts. He was.

"Ananias," he said, without a word of thanks for the money he had brought, "how is it that Satan has so filled your heart that you have lied to the Holy Spirit and have kept for yourself some of the money you received for the land? Didn't it belong to you before it was sold? And after it was sold, wasn't the money at your disposal? What made you think of doing such a thing? You have not lied to men but to God."

So Peter knew what he and his wife had planned in the privacy of their own home! How could he have found out?

Then and there Ananias "fell down and died." Some young men carried out his body and buried it.

Meanwhile, Sapphira was waiting for him to return. What could be keeping him? she wondered. After a while she began to get worried. How could he have taken so long to go so short a distance? Of course, the apostles might have given him some special honor for making such a large donation. After waiting three hours, she thought it was time to look for him.

Peter was still standing at the table, receiving gifts from believers when she entered. Before she could say anything he surprised her by asking, "Tell me, is this the price you and

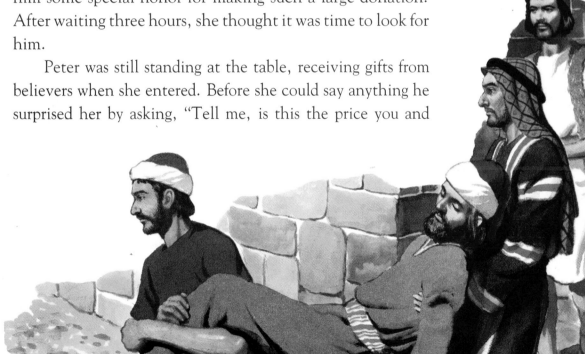

Ananias got for the land?" He mentioned the amount of money Ananias had handed in.

"Yes, that is the price," she said, without a blush.

"How could you agree to test the Spirit of the Lord?" asked Peter.

Before she could answer, he added, "Look! The feet of the men who buried your husband are at the door, and they will carry you out also."

"My husband buried!" I can almost hear her crying. "Ananias dead!"

"At that moment she fell down at his feet and died," and the young men "carried her out and buried her beside her husband."

"Great fear seized the whole church." No wonder! They could see that the Holy Spirit, who had worked such mighty miracles, was not a power to be played with—or lied to.

They saw too the great difference between Barnabas, the son of encouragement, and Ananias, who caused great discouragement. One brought cheer, the other fear. One, by his gracious generosity, blessed the church with happiness. The other, by his selfishness, plunged it into sorrow. Let us decide to be like Barnabas.

Man With the Shining Face

(Acts 6 and 7)

THE DEATH of Ananias and Sapphira struck the first sad note in the story of the early church. But it was not the last. Many more followed, one after another.

First came grumbling. One group of believers thought it was not getting as much money from the general fund as another group. These people said their widows were overlooked while others were given plenty.

I am sure Peter never meant to favor one group above another. He just had too many things to do. Like Moses, he was trying to be a preacher and a teacher, a judge and a businessman, all at the same time, and nobody, not even an apostle, could do so many jobs properly.

Then too, the number of believers was growing every day. The Bible says that they "increased rapidly, and a large number of priests became obedient to the faith." It must have been thrilling to see so many people, even priests, joining the church, but caring for all of them soon became such a big task that the apostles had no time to preach.

31

There were 12 of them again now, for a man called Matthias had been chosen to take the place of Judas. But even so, they couldn't possibly look after the needs of such a large congregation and keep on with their preaching at the same time.

So they called a meeting and said to the believers, "It is not right for us to neglect the preaching of God's word in order to handle finances. So then, brothers, choose seven men among you who are known to be full of the Holy Spirit and wisdom, and he will put them in charge of this matter. We ourselves, then, will give full time to prayer and the work of preaching" (TEV).

The believers were pleased at this suggestion and "chose Stephen, a man full of faith and of the Holy Spirit," and Philip, Procorus, Nicanor, Timon, Parmenas, and Nicolas.

When the election was over, the apostles "prayed and laid their hands on them." These seven men were the first deacons of the Christian church.

Stephen, the head deacon, was a remarkable man. He might have been an apostle if Jesus had met him in Galilee. "Full of God's grace and power," he "did great wonders and miraculous signs among the people."

He was a great speaker, too, and had many discussions with people who said that Christ was not the Messiah. "But they could not stand up against his wisdom or the Spirit by whom he spoke."

What a deacon he was! For a while he took the spotlight from Peter, James, John, and the rest of the apostles. He was such a powerful preacher that the elders and scribes, thinking he must be the ringleader of the followers of Christ, had him arrested and brought before the Sanhedrin.

The charge against him was that he never stopped "speaking against this holy place and against the law," and that he had said "that this Jesus of Nazareth will destroy this place and change the customs Moses handed down to us." It wasn't true, of course. They were just twisting words, as they had done when Christ was in that same place.

As for Stephen, he stood there calmly, without a trace of fear, his heart at peace with God.

"All who were sitting in the Sanhedrin looked intently at Stephen, and they saw that his face was like the face of an angel."

I doubt that any of those councilors had ever seen an angel. But somehow Stephen's face glowed so radiantly with trust and confidence in his beloved Lord and Saviour, that it made them think of angels.

When the high priest asked him whether the charges made against him were true, Stephen defended himself with great power. Showing a marvelous grasp of the Holy Scriptures, he reminded the council how God had led His people from the days of Abraham until that very moment.

He talked of Moses and the deliverance from Egypt, and of

Solomon and the building of the Temple. But when he reminded them that "the Most High does not live in houses made by men," they began to get restless. So he unburdened his heart and told them the straight truth he felt they should hear.

"You stiff-necked people with uncircumcised hearts and ears!" he said. "You are just like your fathers: You always resist the Holy Spirit! Was there ever a prophet your fathers did not persecute? They even killed those who predicted the coming of the Righteous One. And now you have betrayed and murdered him—you who have received the law that was put into effect through angels but have not obeyed it."

The members of the council ground their teeth in anger.

Suddenly, looking up, Stephen cried aloud. " 'Look,' he said, 'I see heaven open and the Son of Man standing at the right hand of God.' "

"Blasphemy!" shrieked the councilors. Covering their ears and "yelling at the top of their voices, they all rushed at him, dragged him out of the city and began to stone him."

As the hail of stones, flung by those cruel and angry men, began to strike him, Stephen fell on his knees and prayed, saying, " 'Lord Jesus, receive my spirit. . . . Lord, do not hold this sin against them.'

"When he had said this, he fell asleep."

So the man with the shining face died. He was the first martyr of the Christian church.

Seeds in the Wind

(Acts 8:1-24)

THE STONING of Stephen was a great shock to the thousands of believers in Jerusalem.

Everything had gone so well that nobody had dreamed anything like this would happen. But now word spread that the Sanhedrin was planning to stamp out the new sect before it could get any stronger. One councilor, a man named Saul of Tarsus, was already going from house to house arresting men and women suspected of being followers of Jesus and putting them in prison.

They were sad days, especially for all the children whose fathers and mothers were taken away to jail. The Bible says that "a great persecution broke out against the church at Jerusalem, and all except the apostles were scattered throughout Judea and Samaria."

Hundreds of Christians fled from the city. Whole families left as quickly as they could. Some went north toward Syria, others south to Egypt. Some took a ship from Caesarea

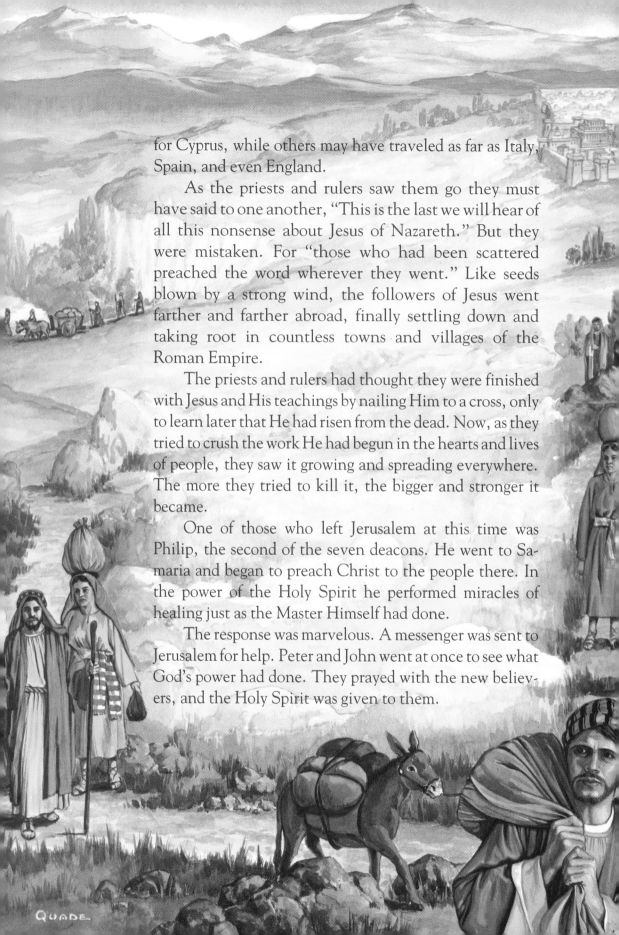

for Cyprus, while others may have traveled as far as Italy, Spain, and even England.

As the priests and rulers saw them go they must have said to one another, "This is the last we will hear of all this nonsense about Jesus of Nazareth." But they were mistaken. For "those who had been scattered preached the word wherever they went." Like seeds blown by a strong wind, the followers of Jesus went farther and farther abroad, finally settling down and taking root in countless towns and villages of the Roman Empire.

The priests and rulers had thought they were finished with Jesus and His teachings by nailing Him to a cross, only to learn later that He had risen from the dead. Now, as they tried to crush the work He had begun in the hearts and lives of people, they saw it growing and spreading everywhere. The more they tried to kill it, the bigger and stronger it became.

One of those who left Jerusalem at this time was Philip, the second of the seven deacons. He went to Samaria and began to preach Christ to the people there. In the power of the Holy Spirit he performed miracles of healing just as the Master Himself had done.

The response was marvelous. A messenger was sent to Jerusalem for help. Peter and John went at once to see what God's power had done. They prayed with the new believers, and the Holy Spirit was given to them.

It must have been hard for some of the Jews to believe that this could happen in Samaria, but it did, right before their eyes, and it was clear proof that Jews and Samaritans could become one in Christ.

The most important convert in Samaria was a man called Simon. He practiced sorcery, and he had had a lot of influence in the city. But now he was nobody, for Philip, Peter, and John worked far greater miracles than he had ever performed.

How he craved the same power they had! He even offered to buy it!

"May your money perish with you," Peter said to him, "because you thought you could buy the gift of God with money! You have no part or share in this ministry, because your heart is not right before God. Repent of this wickedness and pray to the Lord. Perhaps he will forgive you for having such a thought in your heart. For I see that you are full of bitterness and captive to sin."

Simon was repentant. He hadn't understood that there are some things money cannot buy.

"Pray to the Lord for me," he said, "so that nothing you have said may happen to me."

An Old Book Glows

(Acts 8:26-39)

PHILIP was still in Samaria when God sent him on another errand. "Go south to the road—the desert road—that goes down from Jerusalem to Gaza," said the heavenly messenger.

That was all. Just go! So he went.

As he walked along the road, he must have wondered why God wanted him to go to Gaza. Could it be that he was to preach the same message there as he had in Samaria? Or did God have something else in mind?

Soon he heard the familiar cloppety-clop, cloppety-clop, of horses' hooves and the squeaking of wooden wheels and axles.

Looking up, he saw a well-dressed Ethiopian going by in a fine chariot and recognized him as one of the important officials of Candace, queen of Ethiopia. The man was the treasurer of that country. He had been to Jerusalem to worship God in the Temple and was returning home by the desert road.

Suddenly a voice said to Philip, "Go to that chariot and stay near it."

Philip ran, no doubt wondering what to say to this well-to-do stranger.

Seeing Philip running toward him, the Ethiopian told his servant to rein in the horses. As the chariot stopped Philip noticed that the man was reading from a scroll containing the book of Isaiah. So he asked, "Do you understand what you are reading?"

It was a strange question to ask a man he had never met before, but the Ethiopian was not offended. Instead, he invited Philip to get into his chariot and began to ask questions about the text, which says that God's Servant will be "led like a sheep to the slaughter."

"Tell me, please, who is the prophet talking about, himself or someone else?" asked the Ethiopian.

Philip couldn't have wished for a better chance to talk about Jesus. Now he knew why God had told him to walk along the Gaza road! Of course! God had known that this honest seeker after truth would be traveling this way. How

fortunate that Philip had obeyed the call!

"Then Philip began with that very passage of Scripture and told him the good news about Jesus." What a Bible study that must have been!

In a way it was the same Bible study that Jesus had given Cleopas and his friend on the way to Emmaus. Only now it was given by Philip to an Ethiopian on the road to Gaza.

True, Jesus began with Moses, and Philip began with Isaiah. But that didn't matter. They both came to the same conclusion. I am sure there was hardly a prophecy about Jesus in all the Old Testament that Philip left out or a question about Him that the Ethiopian didn't ask.

As the two men journeyed together, the precious old Book they held in their hands glowed with the glory of God. Both felt that the King of glory was speaking directly to them.

And can't you hear Philip saying to the Ethiopian as this wonderful Scripture study drew to a close, "Won't you accept Jesus as *your* Lord and Saviour? Won't you give your heart to Him now?"

"Yes," said the Ethiopian, "I will."

At that moment they happened to pass a pool of water. "Look, here is water," said the Ethiopian. "Why shouldn't I be baptized?"

"You can be," said Philip.

So the Ethiopian "gave orders to stop the chariot. Then both Philip and the eunuch went down into the water and Philip baptized him."

When they came up out of the water, Philip disappeared, taken away by the Spirit of the Lord. The Ethiopian didn't see him again, but he "went on his way rejoicing," to tell the wonderful story of Jesus to his queen and countrymen.

M. deV. Lee

Enemy Becomes a Champion

(Acts 9:1-25)

OF ALL the enemies of the early Christians, the worst was Saul. He was a Pharisee, and he hated the followers of Jesus. The Bible tells us that he "began to destroy the church."

Having done his worst in Jerusalem, he decided to follow those who had left the city and were preaching about Jesus in other parts of the country.

"Saul was still breathing out murderous threats against the Lord's disciples. He went to the high priest and asked him for letters to the synagogues in Damascus, so that if he found any there who belonged to the Way, whether men or women, he might take them as prisoners to Jerusalem."

With his mind full of plans for wiping out the Christians in short order, he started on his journey, leading a group of men who were to help him in his wicked work. For several days they traveled northeastward over the rough, winding roads.

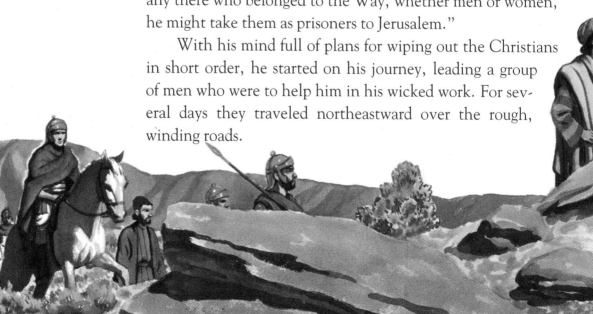

They were almost to Damascus, within sight of the city, when a wonderful thing happened. It was midday. Everybody was hot, tired, and thirsty. Suddenly a light "brighter than the sun" * shone around them. The whole party was struck down. The caravan came to a dead stop.

Blinded by the dazzling light and unable to rise, Saul heard a voice calling to him, "Saul, Saul, why do you persecute Me?"

"Who are You, Lord?" he asked.

"I am Jesus, whom you are persecuting."

Saul was astonished. How could Jesus be here on the Damascus road? Could this be the very Person who the Christians were declaring had risen from the dead? Was He really the King of glory as they claimed? If so, what a dreadful mistake he had

made in treating His followers so cruelly!

A few moments before, Saul had been a proud, self-important man; now he was humble. He saw how foolish he had been.

"What shall I do, Lord?" he asked.

"Get up and go into Damascus," said Jesus. "There you will be told all that you have been assigned to do."

Saul staggered to his feet, while his friends, still trembling with fright, crowded around, offering to help him. But there was nothing they could do except lead him by the hand. He was blind.

When Saul arrived in Damascus, he didn't enter the city striding proudly at the head of a group of men sworn to stamp out the Christian faith, as he had planned. He came stumbling in, humble and penitent, eager to learn the will of Jesus and serve Him faithfully forever.

Saul went to stay with a man called Judas, and there, for three days, he didn't eat or drink. Shocked by what happened to him on the Damascus road and sorry for all his mistakes, he wanted only to pray. On his knees he asked Jesus to forgive him

44

and show him what to do next.

About this time Jesus appeared to Ananias, one of His disciples in Damascus, and said, "Go to the house of Judas on Straight Street and ask for a man from Tarsus named Saul, for he is praying."

Ananias was alarmed. The last person he wanted to meet was Saul. He knew him and all his cruel deeds well. "Lord," Ananias said, "I have heard many reports about this man and all the harm he has done to your saints in Jerusalem."

But Jesus replied, "Go! This man is my chosen instrument to carry my name before the Gentiles and their kings and before the people of Israel."

Ananias obeyed. He found Saul in the home of Judas, praying, as Jesus had said. Putting his hands on him, Ananias said, "Brother Saul, the Lord—Jesus, who appeared to you on the road as you were coming here—has sent me so that you may see again and be filled with the Holy Spirit."

At once Saul's eyes were opened. He could see again. And the first person he saw was a disciple of Jesus, who baptized him into the church.

That was a very lovely thing that Ananias said—"Brother

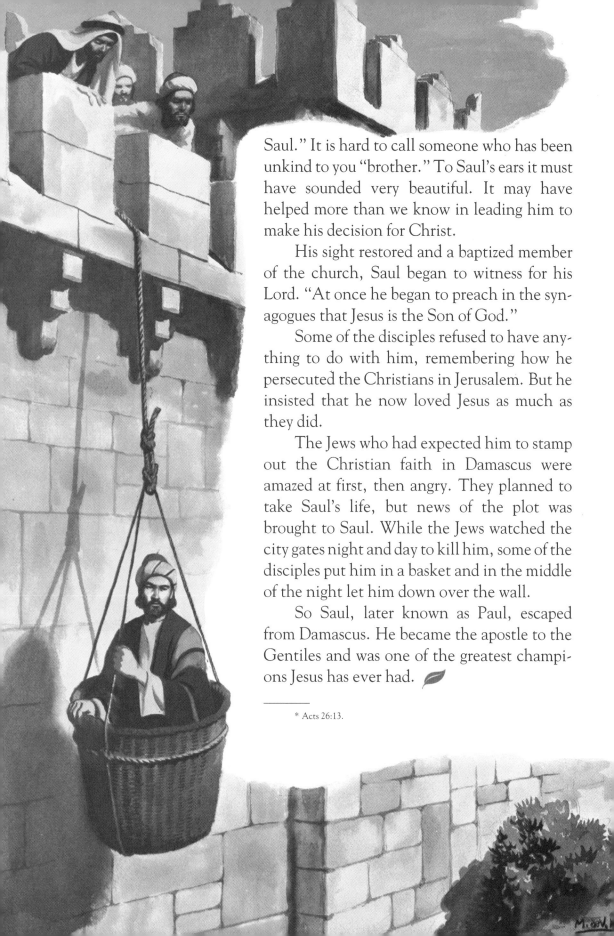

Saul." It is hard to call someone who has been unkind to you "brother." To Saul's ears it must have sounded very beautiful. It may have helped more than we know in leading him to make his decision for Christ.

His sight restored and a baptized member of the church, Saul began to witness for his Lord. "At once he began to preach in the synagogues that Jesus is the Son of God."

Some of the disciples refused to have anything to do with him, remembering how he persecuted the Christians in Jerusalem. But he insisted that he now loved Jesus as much as they did.

The Jews who had expected him to stamp out the Christian faith in Damascus were amazed at first, then angry. They planned to take Saul's life, but news of the plot was brought to Saul. While the Jews watched the city gates night and day to kill him, some of the disciples put him in a basket and in the middle of the night let him down over the wall.

So Saul, later known as Paul, escaped from Damascus. He became the apostle to the Gentiles and was one of the greatest champions Jesus has ever had.

---

* Acts 26:13.

The Antelope Lady

(Acts 9:36-41)

IMAGINE calling a girl an antelope! But that is what her parents did. And that is what she was.

Her real name was Tabitha, meaning "gazelle," or "antelope," or in the Greek language, "Dorcas." And throughout her life she lived up to her name because she was always running as quickly as she could from one needy person to another.

Not only are antelopes swift-footed, but they are gentle and friendly creatures too, and so was Tabitha. Perhaps she had big bright eyes as they do—eyes that showed interest in people and tender sympathy for them in their trials and sorrows.

This wonderful lady was the life of the Joppa church. She was always thinking up new ways of showing kindness to others. The Bible says that she was "always doing good and helping the poor." When she didn't have her hands full nursing somebody's sick child or talking to some blind person or taking flowers to a shut-in, she made clothes for the poor.

47

Yet, though she was busy, she was always patient and sweet-tempered, radiating courage and good cheer everywhere she went. No wonder everybody loved her! No wonder, too, the whole church was plunged into sorrow when she suddenly became ill and died.

Why did she die? I don't know. Possibly because she was worn out helping others. Maybe she caught a germ from some sick person for whom she was caring.

After she died, "her body was washed and placed in an upstairs room."

Somebody said, "If only Peter were here!"

And somebody else said, "But he is!"

"Where?" asked everybody at once.

THE ANTELOPE LADY

"At Lydda, just 10 miles (16 kilometers) away. Only a day or two ago he healed a man named Aeneas, who had been sick in bed for eight years.

"Let's send for him then!" cried everyone, and two men set out for Lydda. Finding Peter, they told him the story of Tabitha and begged him to come at once. He agreed, and the three hurried back to Joppa as fast as they could.

Coming into the room where the body of Dorcas was lying, Peter found it full of weeping widows Dorcas had helped during her lifetime. They showed Peter robes and other clothing she had made for them.

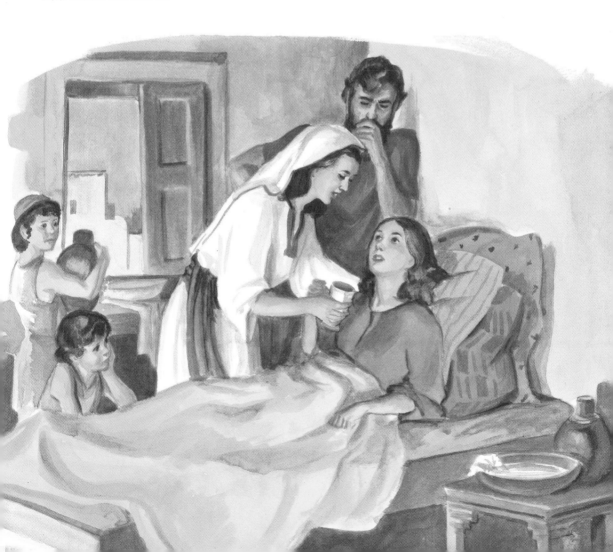

Gently he asked them all to leave. Then he knelt beside the bed and prayed.

What a picture! The big fisherman of Galilee on his knees before God asking Him to give life to a dead woman! How earnestly he must have prayed, just as Elisha prayed for the dead son of the "well-to-do woman" * of Shunem long, long before.

I can almost hear him saying, "Dear Lord, if it be Your will, restore this dear woman to life. Your church in Joppa needs her. Dorcas, they call her, Lord, and that is just what she has been—a gazelle, an antelope, leaping from one good work to another for the sake of Your needy ones. Make it possible for her to continue her ministry of love for the glory of Your name."

As he rose from his knees he turned to the body and said, " 'Tabitha, get up.' She opened her eyes, and seeing Peter she sat up."

THE ANTELOPE LADY

I am sure she did. The last person she would have expected to see in her room was the famous apostle Peter!

And then, of all things, Peter held out his hand to help her up. I am sure she never forgot that simple kindness as long as she lived. And the smile of joy and thankfulness on his noble, friendly face stayed with her forever.

Calling the believers and widows who had been waiting impatiently outside, Peter "presented her to them alive."

They could hardly believe their eyes, and they could hardly contain their happiness. Their dear, kind antelope lady was back with them again!

As for Dorcas, I am sure she didn't stay around very long. In no time at all she went hurrying off to help somebody else who needed her.

---

* 2 Kings 4:8.

Animals in the Sky

(Acts 9:43-10:48)

AFTER bringing Tabitha back to life, Peter stayed on in Joppa in the home of Simon, a tanner. It was here that he had a very strange vision.

It happened one day at noon while he was waiting for lunch. He had gone up on the flat roof of the house to spend a little while in prayer.

He liked this place, not only because from here he could view the sea that he loved so dearly, but because on the house-top there was nothing between him and heaven, where Jesus his Lord and Saviour was sitting at the right hand of God.

He looked up into the sky and thought he saw something strange coming down. It looked like "a large sheet being let down to earth by its four corners." As it came nearer and nearer he saw that the sheet was full of all kinds of animals, reptiles, and birds.

Then a voice said to him, "Get up, Peter. Kill and eat."

Peter was hungry. The Bible says so. But he was not

In his vision Peter saw a great sheet let down from heaven full of all kinds of birds and animals. By this means God taught him that he should call no man common or unclean.

hungry enough for this. The animals were all unclean according to the laws of Moses.

" 'Surely not, Lord!' Peter replied. 'I have never eaten anything impure or unclean.' "

Then the voice spoke again, saying, "Do not call anything impure that God has made clean."

"This happened three times." Then the sheet and the animals went up into the sky again and disappeared.

Peter was troubled by what he had seen. He felt sure he had been given this vision for some purpose, but what was it? Did God want him to eat unclean food? Surely not. There must be some other explanation.

While he was still thinking about all those animals in the sky he heard loud knocking on the gate of the house.

Someone called in a loud voice, "Does Simon Peter live here?"

Peter went to the gate and found three men outside.

"What do you want?" he asked.

They told him that they had come all the way from Caesarea to see him. Cornelius, a famous Roman centurion, had sent them. "Cornelius is a good, God-loving man," they said. "A holy angel told him to have you come to his house so that he could hear what you have to say."

Peter's surprise must have shown on his face. A centurion wanting to see him! What about? He invited the men to come in and stay for the night. In the morning he went off with them to Caesarea.

When they reached the centurion's house, Peter found it crowded with people waiting to see him. He was given a warm welcome, and Cornelius fell on his knees to worship him, as though he were a god.

"Stand up!" said Peter. "I am only a man myself."

By this time he was beginning to understand the meaning of his vision. To the whole group he said, "You are well aware that it is against our law for a Jew to associate with a Gentile or visit him. But God has shown me that I should not call any man impure or unclean. So when I was sent for, I came without raising any objection. May I ask why you sent for me?"

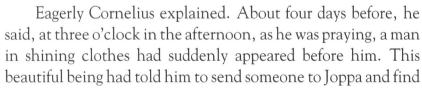

Eagerly Cornelius explained. About four days before, he said, at three o'clock in the afternoon, as he was praying, a man in shining clothes had suddenly appeared before him. This beautiful being had told him to send someone to Joppa and find

a man called Simon Peter, who was living as "a guest in the home of Simon the tanner, who lives by the sea."

"The man in shining clothes seemed to know exactly where you lived," said Cornelius, "so I sent for you immediately, and it was good of you to come. Now we are all here in the presence of God to listen to everything the Lord has commanded you to tell us."

This was a great lesson to Peter. Up to this moment he had thought that the kingdom of God was only for Jews, but he saw how wrong and foolish this idea was. "I now realize how true it is that God does not show favoritism," he said, "but accepts men from every nation who fear him and do what is right."

Then he began to talk about Jesus "and how he went around doing good and healing all who were under the power of the devil."

"I was there," he said. "I was with Him all the time from the early days in Galilee until He was crucified. I saw Him after

55

He arose from the dead. We ate and drank together."

It was just a simple, personal testimony, but Cornelius and the rest of the people in the room listened spellbound.

"He commanded us to preach to the people," Peter went on, "and to testify that he is the one whom God appointed as judge of the living and the dead. All the prophets testify about him that everyone who believes in him receives forgiveness of sins through his name."

Hour after hour he talked, and everybody was convinced by his words. They accepted Jesus as their Saviour without question.

Then something wonderful happened. "While Peter was still speaking . . . , the Holy Spirit came on all who heard the message," and they began to praise and glorify God.

Some Jews who were present were shocked. They couldn't understand how God could pour out His Spirit on Gentiles. But Peter did. Those animals in the sky had told him.

"Can anyone," he asked, "keep these people from being baptized with water? They have received the Holy Spirit just as we have."

Of course nobody could. And nobody did. God had spoken. These godly Gentiles were just as dear to Him as any of the children of Abraham.

They were all baptized, and a Roman centurion became a member of the Christian church.

Prison Doors Open

(Acts 12:1-19)

B Y THIS time the little company of fire-filled disciples who had hurried out of the meeting place on the day of Pentecost had become a large number of believers. After the conversion of Saul persecution stopped for a while, and thousands accepted the gospel. The Bible says that "a great number of people believed and turned to the Lord."

But the good times did not last long.

King Herod arrested James, the brother of John, and put him to death. Because he saw this pleased the Jewish leaders, he put Peter in prison, intending to kill him after the Passover.

Herod had been told that Peter had escaped from prison once before, so he gave orders that "four squads of four soldiers each" should guard him day and night. Peter wouldn't get out this time!

Meanwhile, the disciples in Jerusalem, having seen James executed, were terribly worried about their beloved Peter. Would he suffer the same dreadful fate?

From early morning till late at night, yes, and all through

57

the night, they prayed for him. "O Jesus, please save Peter," they cried. "Don't let them kill our dear Peter!"

Day after day, night after night, Peter remained in the prison, while the church pleaded for his release. But nothing happened. The last night came, the night before he was to die. He would be executed the next morning. Would God deliver him?

Chained in his dungeon, Peter thought back over his past life, how he had first met Jesus in Galilee, how he had followed Him for more than three years and then, in the last crisis, had denied Him. He remembered how he had said angrily, "I don't know the man!" * and then the rooster had crowed. Had Jesus forgiven him for that? Would He come and save him now?

It seemed impossible. What could anyone do at this late hour? Peter looked at the chains on his hands and feet, the two soldiers in his cell, the locked door, the soldiers outside, the huge iron gate at the entrance to the prison. What hope of escape was there? Who could possibly rescue him from such a place?

He was sleeping between two soldiers when suddenly he

58

felt a blow on his side. He sat up, wondering who had struck him and why.

Now a hand was grasping his and pulling him to his feet. "Quick, get up!" whispered a voice.

Mysteriously his chains dropped off, clanking loudly on the stone floor.

"Put on your clothes and sandals," said the stranger.

Peter obeyed, dressing as quickly as he could. Then the stranger spoke again. "Wrap your cloak around you and follow me," he said.

Silently the stranger opened the cell door and passed through it, Peter following, wondering whether he was dreaming.

Past the first guard they went, past the second, then into the courtyard. All was still, except for the dull snoring of the soldiers, who seemed to be dead asleep.

Ahead loomed the massive iron gate. Beyond it was the city and freedom. Could they get through? Did this stranger have the key?

As they approached the gate, to Peter's amazement, it opened all by itself.

They went through the gate and down to the end of the street. Peter turned to thank the stranger who had rescued him, but no one was there. "Now I know without a doubt," he said to himself, "that the Lord sent his angel and rescued me from Herod's clutches and from everything the Jewish people were anticipating."

Thankful for his cloak so that he could hide his face from anyone on the street, Peter hurried through the darkened city to the house of Mary, the mother of John Mark, where many disciples were gathered in prayer for him.

He knocked on the door, and,

to make sure that the people inside would not be afraid to open it, he called out his name.

A girl named Rhoda came to open the door and recognized Peter's voice. She was so happy to think Peter was out there that she forgot to let him in, and she ran back into the room where the prayer meeting was still going on.

"Peter's here—outside the door!" she cried. "I heard his voice."

"You're out of your mind!" they said to her.

"But I heard him!" she said. "I know it is Peter."

Still they refused to believe.

Meanwhile, Peter was getting impatient, afraid that he might be discovered out there on the street. He went on knocking.

At last all of them went to the door and opened it. And there he stood. They could hardly believe their eyes.

"Peter!" they cried. "Is it really you?" and they gave him such a welcome that he had to beg them to be quiet so the soldiers would not be alerted and come and find him there. Then he told them the wonderful story of how an angel had rescued him from the prison.

By morning all Jerusalem had heard the exciting news. From one to another the word spread like wildfire, "Peter has escaped again!" Tongues wagged, and people from one end of the city to the other chuckled.

Down at the prison there was "no small commotion" over the missing prisoner. No wonder, with all those soldiers supposed to be guarding him! But nobody had seen anything. Nobody had heard anything. He had just disappeared.

Herod was furious, but what could he do but call off the execution? There was no one to execute!

As for Peter, a great thankfulness filled his heart. Once more His beloved Jesus had rescued him. With new courage and hope he went out to do an even greater work for the King of glory he adored.

_____
* Matthew 26:74.

PART TWO

Stories of

the First
Christian
Missionaries

(Acts 13:1-28:31)

Saul Becomes Paul

(Acts 13:1-12)

AS TROUBLE grew worse in Jerusalem more and more people who believed in Jesus moved away to other cities. Many went to Antioch in Syria, about 300 miles (480 kilometers) to the north, where they found a warm welcome.

In no time at all they were telling their new friends all about the beloved Carpenter of Nazareth, and they too accepted Christ.

When this wonderful news reached the apostles, they asked Barnabas to go to Antioch and find out what was going on. His friendly nature made him just the right person to send on such a mission. What he found made him very happy, and he was such an encouragement to the new believers and others in the community, that many more were "brought to the Lord."

About this time Barnabas became worried about Saul, who had disappeared. A true "son of encouragement," Barnabas traveled as far as Tarsus—about 100 miles (160 kilometers) northwest—in his search for him. When he found Saul, he

At Antioch, where the disciples were first called Christians, Saul and Barnabas and Mark were ordained as missionaries to carry the gospel to Cyprus and lands across the sea.

asked him to come and help strengthen the new church he had raised up in Antioch.

Saul agreed. And so began the wonderful partnership of these two good men, which brought so much blessing to so many.

Those must have been great days in Antioch. The Bible says that the disciples were first called Christians there. No doubt the kindly spirit of Barnabas and the forceful preaching of Saul had much to do with it. Both of them uplifted Christ so much that people wanted to belong to Him and to be known as His followers.

One day the presence of God was felt in the church in a very special way. The Holy Spirit sent this message: "Set apart for me Barnabas and Saul for the work to which I have called them."

There was no mistaking what God wanted. These two men, who had been such a help to the Antioch church, were now to go and preach the good tidings of Jesus' love to others.

This was something new in those days, and I imagine everyone was excited as they planned for the great adventure. The church members could talk of nothing else. Their beloved pastors were going to travel to distant places to establish other Christian churches on the island of Cyprus and all through Asia Minor! Young John Mark, who was a cousin of Barnabas, would go along as their assistant. How big and important this adventure must have seemed to them!

At last it was time for the farewell meeting. After fasting and praying, the church members laid their hands on Saul and

Barnabas and sent them off. I am sure that crowds went down to the docks at Seleucia to wave goodbye as the ship sailed out of the harbor. Mothers and fathers, boys and girls, were all there for the great occasion.

As they shouted their last good wishes and waved to the three lonely figures standing on the deck of that little vessel I wonder whether any of them realized that they were sending off the first overseas missionaries. Paul, Barnabas, and John Mark began the long line of God's messengers who would go abroad to preach the gospel.

A few hours later the travelers arrived at Salamis, a port on the east coast of Cyprus. As soon as they had found a place to stay they went first to one synagogue, then to another, telling the story of Jesus to the Jewish leaders. Then they journeyed on across the island until they came to the city of Paphos, on the west coast. Here they ran into quite a bit of excitement.

After they had been in town awhile, Sergius Paulus, the Roman proconsul or governor, sent for them. He was curious about these strangers and the things they were talking about. He wanted them to explain their message to him. They were glad to, and Sergius Paulus, "an intelligent man," became very interested. Barnabas and Saul could see that he was on the verge of accepting Jesus as his Saviour.

Then came an interruption.

"Don't believe them!" cried a sneering voice. "What they are saying is all nonsense."

It was Elymas, a local sorcerer who was keen enough to see that if the proconsul accepted what these preachers were saying, he wouldn't want a sorcerer around anymore. But he soon wished he had kept quiet.

Saul turned on him with burning words of rebuke. He was angry that anyone should get in God's way like this and try to keep this fine Roman officer out of the kingdom.

"You are a child of the devil," he said to Elymas, "and an enemy of everything that is right! You are full of all kinds of deceit and trickery. Will you never stop perverting the right ways of the Lord? Now the hand of the Lord is against you. You are going to be blind, and for a time you will be unable to see the light of the sun."

Barely had Saul spoken when his words came true.

"I can't see! I can't see!" cried Elymas, putting his hands to his eyes. "Immediately mist and darkness came over him, and he groped about, seeking someone to lead him by the hand."

Deeply impressed, the proconsul gave his heart to God, "for he was amazed at the teaching about the Lord."

As for Saul, something happened to him too. Just how, we are not told. But from this moment on the Bible calls him Paul.

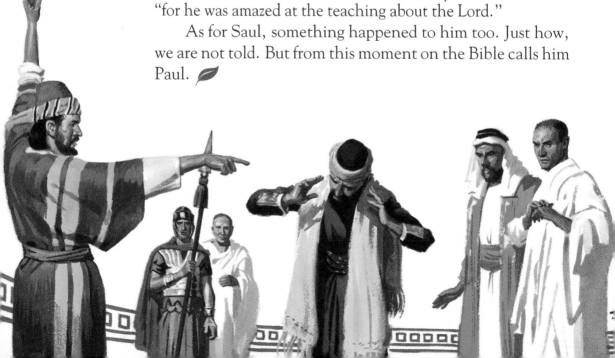

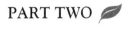

Mistaken for Gods

(Acts 13:13-14:20)

SAILING from Paphos, the three missionaries reached the mainland again at Perga in Asia Minor. Here John Mark said goodbye to Paul and Barnabas and left for home. Maybe he got too sick on that last boat trip, or perhaps he couldn't stand the hardships of travel in those days. Anyway, he packed up and returned to Jerusalem, much to Paul's disappointment.

The two older men went on alone and came to Pisidian Antioch. Paul was invited to speak in the synagogue, and he preached a great sermon, proving that Jesus is not only the son of David but the Son of God. "Through Jesus," he declared, "the forgiveness of sins is proclaimed to you."

After the meeting the Gentiles outside asked him to preach the same sermon to them. He did. "On the next Sabbath almost the whole city gathered to hear the word of the Lord."

This upset the Jews. They didn't want to share anything with the Gentiles. Not even a good preacher. So they became

ROME

THREE TAVERNS
APPII FORUM

PUTEOLI

ITALY

MACEDONIA

AMPHIPOL

THESSALONICA

BEREA

SICILY

RHEGIUM

GREECE

CORINTH

ATHE

SYRACUSE

CENCHREA

MALTA

C R

LA

T H E

N
W   E
S

G R E A T

(MEDITERRANEAN)

LIBYA

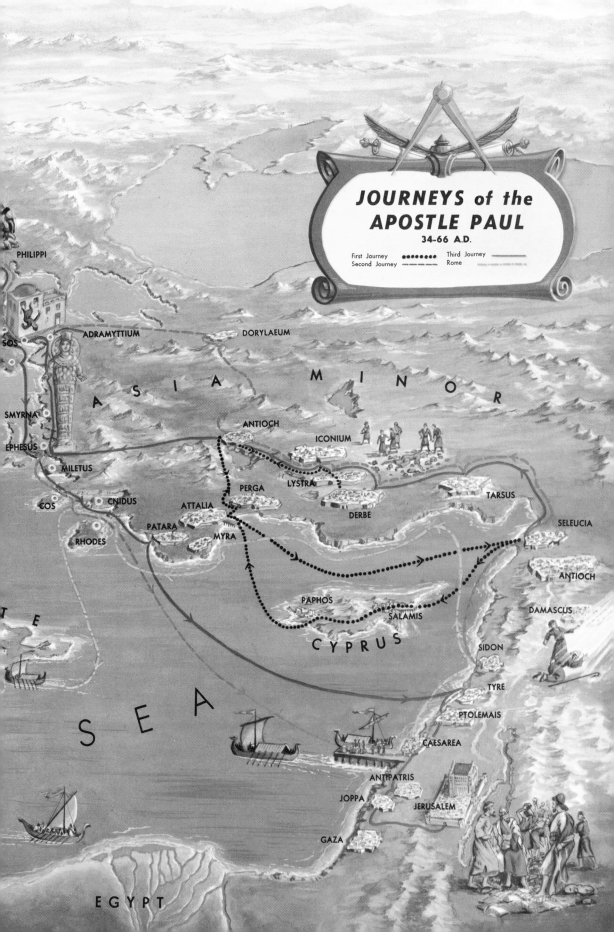

JOURNEYS of the APOSTLE PAUL

34-66 A.D.

First Journey ●●●●●●●
Second Journey − − − − −
Third Journey ————
Rome ————

PHILIPPI

ADRAMYTTIUM   DORYLAEUM

SOS

A S I A   M I N O R

SMYRNA

ANTIOCH   ICONIUM

EPHESUS

MILETUS   PERGA   LYSTRA   TARSUS

ATTALIA   DERBE   SELEUCIA

COS   CNIDUS

PATARA   ANTIOCH

RHODES   MYRA

DAMASCUS

PAPHOS   SALAMIS

C Y P R U S   SIDON

TYRE

PTOLEMAIS

E   CAESAREA

S E A   ANTIPATRIS

JOPPA   JERUSALEM

GAZA

E G Y P T

angry with Paul and Barnabas and began to find fault with them and their message.

In the middle of the hubbub, Paul said to them, "We had to speak the word of God to you first. Since you reject it and do not consider yourselves worthy of eternal life, we now turn to the Gentiles."

This pleased the Gentiles, and many of them accepted Jesus as their Saviour. But the Jews stirred up so much trouble that Paul and Barnabas finally had to leave town.

The two missionaries went to Iconium and started all over again. Soon this city too was stirred from one end to the other. A great many people, both Jews and Gentiles, became Christians. But this annoyed the others who didn't join the

church, and soon the whole place was divided between those who were for the visiting preachers and those who were against them.

Things got so bad that a plot was laid to take their lives. Learning of it in time, Paul and Barnabas left for Lystra, where they preached in peace for a while.

Then one day as Paul was speaking, he noticed a man in the audience who was "crippled in his feet." The poor man had been lame from birth, and as he listened to the story of the love and power of Jesus he looked up longingly. Guessing what was going on in the man's mind, and seeing that "he had faith to be healed," Paul called to him in a loud voice, "Stand up on your feet!"

Instantly the man "jumped up and began to walk," to the amazement of everybody around.

Like wildfire the report of the miracle spread. People from all over town came running to see the healed man and the men who had made him well.

"The gods have come down to us in human form!" they cried. "Barnabas they called Zeus, and Paul they called Hermes because he was the chief speaker." Then the priest of the temple of Zeus "brought bulls and wreaths" and prepared to offer sacrifices to the two visiting "gods."

Paul and Barnabas were shocked. The last thing they wanted was to be worshiped as pagan gods! Running into the crowd, they cried, "Don't do this! We are not gods! We are

only men, just like you. We have come to tell you about the
living God, who made heaven and earth, and the sea and
everything that is in them; who gives the rain and the seasons
and satisfies your hearts with food and gladness."

"Even with these words," the Bible says, "they had dif-
ficulty keeping the crowd from sacrificing to them."

At last the people saw that they had been mistaken.
Gradually the shouting died down, and the priests took the
bulls and wreaths back to their temple.

In place of the excitement came disappointment. Those
who had been loudest in their praise of Paul and Barnabas
now began to criticize them. Unfortunately, some travelers
arrived from Antioch and Iconium who accused the two
missionaries of being frauds and impostors. This was all the

crowd needed to turn once more into a howling mob. Now, instead of wanting to worship Paul and Barnabas, the people tried to kill them.

Barnabas escaped, but Paul was stoned.

Thinking he was dead, the crowd dragged him out of the gates and left his poor, bruised body on the city dump.

But it took more than this to kill Paul. As some of the new believers gathered around to pay their last respects, he opened his eyes, stood up, and went right back into Lystra! What courage! What holy boldness!

Paul was no pagan god, but truly a God-filled man.

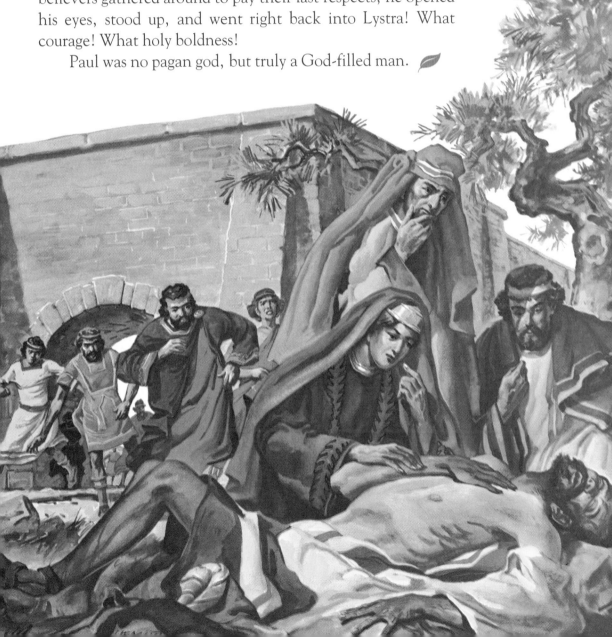

Big Argument Settled

(Acts 14:20-15:31)

THE NEXT day Paul and Barnabas set off for the nearby city of Derbe. After working here for a while, the two returned to Lystra, then to Iconium, and back to Pisidian Antioch.

In each of these cities they met with the new disciples, urging them to "remain true to the faith" and explaining to them that "we must go through many hardships to enter the kingdom of God." They also ordained elders in every church and prayed with them.

So they returned to Perga and sailed from the nearby port of Attalia to Seleucia and so to Antioch in Syria, where they had started their journey. You can see where they went by looking at the map on pages 70 and 71.

What a welcome they received! The whole church came together to hear their report. Those who had waved goodbye to them months before now listened eagerly as the two missionaries "reported all that God had done through them and how he had opened the door of faith to the Gentiles."

They had traveled about 2,400 miles (3,860 kilometers) in all, which was a long way in those days. And what a story they had to tell! Everybody was thrilled as they heard about Sergius Paulus and Elymas, about the poor crippled man at Lystra, about Paul and Barnabas being mistaken for gods, about Paul being stoned and left for dead and how he got up and walked back into the city.

Best of all was the news that the preaching of the gospel had done its life-changing work as wonderfully in one place as another and had touched the hearts of Gentiles and Jews alike. Many of the boys and girls in the congregation must have said, "When I grow up, I'm going to be a missionary too."

Strangely, not all who listened to them were pleased with their report. Some argued that before Gentiles could become Christians they must become like Jews and keep all the laws that Moses gave the Israelites in the desert.

"No!" said Paul, putting his foot down. "That's all wrong. Christ does not require any such thing of His disciples."

The two views were held so strongly that at last the apostles called a big committee meeting to talk it over. It was the first general council of the Christian church.

Paul and Barnabas were chosen to go to Jerusalem and tell their story to the believers there. On the way they stopped at various churches and "told how the Gentiles had been con-

verted. This news made all the brothers very glad."

Arriving at Jerusalem, they were given another warm welcome by the church, the apostles, and the elders. Paul and Barnabas "reported everything God had done through them."

James was the chairman, and he gave the members all the time they needed to discuss their views. Peter got up and reminded the assembly how God had poured out His Holy Spirit on both Jews and Gentiles alike and put no difference between them. "We believe it is through the grace of our Lord Jesus that we are saved," he said, "just as they are."

Then Barnabas and Paul told "about the miraculous signs and wonders God had done among the Gentiles through them."

When they had finished, James gave the final decision. "It is my judgment, therefore," he said, "that we should not make it difficult for the Gentiles who are turning to God. Instead we should write to them, telling them to abstain from food polluted by idols, from sexual immorality, from the meat of strangled animals and from blood."

The council wrote a letter describing this decision and sent it out to the churches.

It was a great forward step. Not only did the council settle a big argument but it opened wide the doors of the Christian church to everybody. From now on men and women among every race and tribe around the globe would know they were welcome. Membership was as free as the love of God.

Singing in Jail

(Acts 15:36-16:25)

SOMETIME after Paul and Barnabas had returned to Antioch, they decided to revisit the churches they had raised up in Asia Minor.

Paul suggested, "Let us go back and visit the brothers in all the towns where we preached the word of the Lord and see how they are doing."

Barnabas said he would be happy to go and that it would be nice to take John Mark along too, as they had before.

"John Mark!" objected Paul. "Not that young man! He may be your cousin, but I'll never take *him* again. He got scared and ran home."

"Let's give him another chance!" pleaded Barnabas, the "son of encouragement."

"No!" said Paul, "*not* John Mark."

How long they argued we do not know, but the Bible says "they had such a sharp disagreement that they parted company."

It was too bad, for the churches' members would have loved

to see both of them again. But Barnabas would not desert his young cousin, and so he sailed with him to Cyprus. Paul chose Silas as his new companion, and they "went through Syria and Cilicia, strengthening the churches."

As it turned out, Barnabas was right. John Mark proved to be a valuable and trustworthy worker. In later years even Paul came to speak of him as a fellow worker "for the kingdom of God" and "a comfort to me." [1] And just before his death he wrote, "He is helpful to me in my ministry." [2]

So it pays to give boys—and girls—another chance!

Traveling on from church to church, Paul and Silas came to Lystra, where Paul had been stoned and left for dead on his previous trip. Among those waiting to welcome him were young Timothy, his mother, Eunice, and his grandmother, Lois, all of whom had accepted Jesus when he was there before. How glad they must have been to see him again! Yes, and how glad Paul must have been that he had gone to Lystra in the first place, despite all he suffered there.

Eager to spread the gospel farther and farther, Paul tried to enter other parts of Asia Minor, but for one reason or another he was unable to do so. There was always something in the way. He wondered why. Then one night he found out.

He was at Troas, a port on the Aegean Sea, where ships departed constantly for various ports in Europe. As he slept he saw in vision a man dressed in the costume of the Macedonians,

who said, "Come over to Macedonia and help us."

In the morning Paul told Silas what he had seen and heard, and they both took it to be a call from God. That very day they went down to the docks and arranged to travel on a ship going to Neapolis. From there they went to Philippi, which at that time was "the leading city of that district of Macedonia."

As they looked for an opportunity to win someone to Christ they learned that some of the religious women of the church went every Sabbath to a place of prayer by the river. Paul and Silas decided to go and worship with them. As a result, Lydia, a "dealer in purple cloth," accepted Jesus as her Saviour and was baptized. She invited Paul and Silas to stay in her home, which they were glad to do.

This led to the conversion of another woman and lots of trouble.

One day, as Paul and Silas were on their way to the prayer meeting, a slave girl passed by calling out, "These men are servants of the Most High God, who are telling you the way to be saved."

The two men were astonished. How did this poor, uneducated girl know so much? But as she kept on saying the same words over and over again, they decided that she must be possessed by an evil spirit. Her owners used her to make lots of money by fortune-telling.

Stopping the girl, Paul spoke to the evil spirit, saying, "In the name of Jesus Christ I command you to come out of her!" The spirit obeyed, and the girl was left in her right mind, thankful to be free again.

But her owners weren't thankful. They were angry. Their source of easy money was gone, and they rushed Paul and Silas to the local judges, charging them with being troublemakers and teaching customs that were offensive to the Roman people.

There was no fair trial, and Paul and Silas had no chance to defend themselves. Soon everybody was shouting insults at them. The judges ruled them guilty and ordered that they should be beaten and put in prison.

So their clothes were torn off, and they were publicly beaten and taken to prison. Here they were placed in the inner cell, and their feet were fastened in the stocks.

It was enough to crush anybody's spirit. But not Paul's or Silas'. They might have asked, "Why did God let this happen to us when we were working for Him?" But they didn't. Instead, despite the pain of their bruised and bleeding backs, they prayed and sang hymns to God.

Hearing their happy voices, the other prisoners were amazed. Singing in jail! What a thing to do! No grumbling, only thanksgiving. What wonderful men they must have been! No wonder God loved them so. No wonder He shook the earth to set them free!

---

[1] Colossians 4:10, 11.
[2] 2 Timothy 4:11.

The Wound Washer

(Acts 16:26-40)

S UDDENLY, about midnight, while Paul and Silas were still singing, "there was such a violent earthquake that the foundations of the prison were shaken. At once all the prison doors flew open, and everybody's chains came loose."

Awaking from sleep, the jailer rushed from his bed to find out what had happened. In the darkness he couldn't see much—just piles of debris on the floor and the dungeon doors swinging wide open.

Fearing that his prisoners had run away and knowing he would be blamed for their escape, he drew his sword to kill himself. Paul cried out, "Don't harm yourself! We are all here!"

"A light!" cried the jailer. "Bring a light!"

A servant came running with a torch. The jailer made his way into the inner cell and fell on his knees before Paul and Silas. He had heard these men praying and singing, and he knew in his heart that they had been beaten and jailed

85

unjustly. He also knew that they had something he did not have—peace of mind.

As he led them out of the inner cell, he said, "Sirs, what must I do to be saved?"

This was an unusual question for a jailer to ask his prisoners, but Paul and Silas were ready with an answer. They saw another chance to tell the gospel story.

"Believe in the Lord Jesus," they said, "and you will be saved—you and your household."

The man knew little or nothing about Jesus. So he took Paul and Silas into his home so he could learn what they meant by these strange words.

The two preachers weren't very presentable. Their clothes were torn, their backs bloodstained, their hands unwashed, their beards untidy. So the jailer did his best to fix them up and make them comfortable, while Paul and Silas went on talking.

First of all, the jailer washed their wounds. That was a beautiful thing for him to do. He wanted to make right the

86

wrong that had been done to these good men, and this was the best way he knew how to do it.

What a wonderful lesson for us! If we injure somebody by what we say or do, it's not enough just to say, "I'm sorry." We must wash the wounds and do what we can to make them better.

Boys and girls are often all too quick to hurt others and all too slow to wash the wounds they make. They will gang up on other children at school and make fun of their clothes, their lunches, their parents, or perhaps the color of their skin. They never think of the pain they cause or the need for someone to help heal the wounds. Sometimes cruel things are said or done at home, and a little brother or sister feels this unkindness in his or her heart.

The world needs more wound washers today. So does your church, your school, your family.

By morning the jailer of Philippi had been baptized, together with his wife and children. What a night that was! It began with a beating and ended with a baptism, with an earthquake thrown in for good measure.

Then the officers arrived with a message from the

magistrates to say that Paul and Silas were free to leave the prison.

"Oh, no," said Paul. "They beat us publicly without a trial, even though we are Roman citizens, and threw us into prison. And now do they want to get rid of us quietly? No! Let them come themselves and escort us out."

Now it was the magistrates' turn to be worried. To beat a Roman citizen without a proper trial was a serious offense in those days. Learning what Paul had said, they came hurrying to the prison to apologize. Politely they begged the two men to leave town as soon as possible.

Paul and Silas accepted the apology, but they were in no hurry to leave Philippi. From the prison they went to see their friend Lydia and to talk with the other new believers. Then, in their own good time, they went on their way to Thessalonica, where more exciting events awaited them.

Turning the World Upside Down

(Acts 17:1-10)

FROM Philippi Paul and Silas went to Thessalonica, or Thessaloniki, as it is called today. This meant a journey of almost 100 miles (160 kilometers), and it probably took several days, allowing for stops on the way.

By the time the two missionaries arrived in Thessalonica, they had recovered from the beating they had been given in jail and were all ready to preach again.

They found a place to stay in the home of a man called Jason. Then, "as his custom was, Paul went into the synagogue, and on three Sabbath days he reasoned with them from the Scriptures, explaining and proving that the Christ had to suffer and rise from the dead. 'This Jesus I am proclaiming to you is the Christ,' he said."

For a while all went well. Some Jews believed and accepted Jesus as their Saviour. Many Greeks believed also, "and not a few prominent women."

Paul and Silas must have been very happy at this fine result of their preaching. But their joy did not last very long. Soon

89

some of the Jews, who refused to believe that Jesus was the Messiah, charged that the two men were frauds and cheats and should be driven out of town. Gathering a crowd, they "started a riot in the city."

Arriving at Jason's house, they demanded that Paul and Silas be handed over to them. But the apostles weren't there. Perhaps they had slipped out the back door when they saw the angry crowd coming down the street.

Angered because they couldn't find the men they were looking for, the leaders of the mob seized Jason and rushed him off to the city magistrates.

"These people who have been turning the world upside down have come here also," they cried, "and Jason has entertained them as guests. They are all acting contrary to the decrees of the emperor, saying that there is another king named Jesus" (NRSV).

There was a good deal of fuss and argument, but finally Jason was set free after he had posted a bond for his good behavior. Returning home, he got word to Paul and Silas that it would be best for them to leave town for a while. That night the two set out for Berea, some 50 miles (80 kilometers) toward the southwest.

As they trudged on through the darkness, they must have smiled as they thought of what their enemies had said about them that day. I can almost hear Paul saying, "So they think we have been 'turning the world upside down' with the good news about Jesus! We wish we had!"

Once more they were running for their lives, looking back now and then to see whether they were being pursued and wondering whether they would arrive safely in Berea.

Many people had accepted their message in Thessalonica, but how few they were compared with the crowds who had rejected it! Both Paul and Silas wished they could have stayed longer and done more. It was too bad they had had to leave so soon. As for "turning the world upside down," that is just what Jesus had sent them to do.

Day after day, in city after city, they were planting ideas in people's minds that would change their lives completely. They would be "turned upside down" and never be the same again. Neither would the world in which they lived.

That's what the gospel of Jesus does. It turns people's lives upside down. It changes their likes and dislikes. It changes their motives and ambitions. Instead of loving the world and hating God, they love God and hate the world. Instead of being proud, they become humble. Instead of being irritable, they become patient. Instead of wanting to please themselves, they try their best to please Jesus. Their whole outlook on life is "turned upside down."

And that's what Jesus will do for you if you receive Him into your heart.

Seekers After Truth

(Acts 17:11-18:22)

A RRIVING in Berea, Paul and Silas began once more to preach about Jesus, and here they ran across something very encouraging.

As they spoke in the synagogue they noticed how eager the people were to learn the truth. They brought out the ancient scrolls and examined them carefully. The Bible says that "the Bereans were of more noble character than the Thessalonians, for they received the message with great eagerness and examined the Scriptures every day to see if what Paul said was true."

The people probably held meetings in their homes as well as in the synagogue, earnestly studying the Bible. As a result, many of the Jews came to believe in Jesus, and so did "a number of prominent Greek women and many Greek men."

When word got back to Thessalonica about what was happening, the Jews who had caused trouble there hurried over to Berea and tried to undo the good work the Christian missionaries had begun. To avoid trouble, Paul went to Athens, leaving Silas and Timothy to strengthen the new disciples in the faith.

93

← PAINTING BY RUSSELL HARLAN

The Bereans were more responsive to the gospel than the people of Thessalonica because they recognized the authority of God's Word and studied its counsels daily for instruction.

Boarding a ship, Paul sailed for the famous center of learn-ing for Greece, which he had often longed to see. But he was disappointed. The city was full of idols, and nobody took much notice of his preaching.

"What is this babbler trying to say?" they asked with a sneer. When Paul tried to discuss the Scriptures with them, they laughed at him.

On Mars' Hill, where the people of Athens gathered to discuss the news, he tried to interest them in the greatest news of all—that the invisible God had made Himself visible in Jesus, and that, though He had been crucified by wicked men, He had risen from the dead. This Jesus, he said, was alive and would one day "judge the world with justice."

94

The result was disappointing. "When they heard about the resurrection of the dead, some of them sneered, but others said, 'We want to hear you again on this subject.' " Only a very few believed.

So Paul went on to Corinth, no doubt wondering whether he would have the same experience in that big city as he had had in Athens. Arriving in town, he became acquainted with a Jew named Aquila and his wife, Priscilla. They were tentmakers, and since this was Paul's trade too, they were soon good friends.

As usual, Paul began his work by visiting the synagogues, but he had a hard time. Fierce arguments developed. He was so bitterly opposed that at last he said to the Jewish leaders, "Your blood be on your own heads! I am clear of my responsibility. From now on I will go to the Gentiles."

It was very discouraging. Paul must have asked himself many times whether it was worthwhile trying to preach the gospel to such people. Then one night the Lord Jesus spoke to him in a vision. "Do not be afraid," He said; "keep on speaking, do not be silent. For I am with you, and no one is going to attack and harm you, because I have many people in this city."

Greatly cheered, Paul stayed on in Corinth for another 18 months, "teaching them the word of God."

And the Lord kept His promise. Many people accepted

Paul's message, and the Corinthian church was formed. When trouble finally came and "the Jews made a united attack on Paul," he was protected from harm by the chief judge.

As he stood before the Roman proconsul Gallio, charged with "persuading the people to worship God in ways contrary to the law," he must have wondered whether he would be condemned or released. But the Lord had said he would not be harmed in Corinth, and he wasn't.

Turning on the men who had brought the charge against Paul, Gallio said, " 'If you Jews were making a complaint about some misdemeanor or serious crime, it would be reasonable for me to listen to you. But since it involves questions about words and names and your own law—settle the matter yourselves. I will not be a judge of such things.' So he had them ejected from the court."

Paul was released. Saying goodbye to the new Corinthian Christians, he left by ship for Syria, taking with him his good friends the tentmakers Aquila and Priscilla.

After a brief visit to the church at Ephesus, where he left his two friends, he sailed on to Caesarea. From here he went by road to Jerusalem, and then back to his old home church at Antioch. What a story he had to tell when he got there!

Seven Foolish Brothers

(Acts 18:23-19:16)

AFTER spending some time in Antioch, Paul became restless again. He wanted to visit the churches he had raised up on his two previous missionary journeys. So "Paul set out from there and traveled from place to place throughout the region of Galatia and Phrygia, strengthening all the disciples."

How glad the new believers must have been to see him again! There was no radio then, no television, no daily mail service that could deliver messages of cheer from their beloved leader. They received letters from him on only the rarest occasions. Seldom, if ever, did they hear any preacher other than their own church elder. Now here was Paul again, in person! I am sure they welcomed him with tears of joy.

Eventually Paul came again to Ephesus. Wonderful things began to happen. For three months he spoke in the synagogue "arguing persuasively about the kingdom of God." Then, when some in his audience became troublesome, he rented the lecture hall of Tyrannus and spoke there every day for two years.

Thousands came to hear him, for we read that "all the Jews and Greeks who lived in the province of Asia heard the word of the Lord."

And it was not only Paul's preaching that impressed the people so much. They were amazed at the way he healed the sick. The Bible tells us that "God did extraordinary miracles through Paul, so that even handkerchiefs and aprons that had touched him were taken to the sick, and their illnesses were cured and the evil spirits left them."

In the audience one day were seven sons of a Jewish priest named Sceva. They noticed that whenever Paul spoke to some poor sick man or woman and said, "In the name of Jesus Christ of Nazareth, be well"—or words like that—the sick person got well immediately. Thinking there must be some magic in Paul's words, they decided to find out whether the same words would work for them.

Seeing a man in the crowd who evidently was possessed by an evil spirit, one of them said to him, "In the name of Jesus, whom Paul preaches, I command you to come out."

Nothing happened—at least not what the young men expected. Instead "the evil spirit answered them, 'Jesus I know, and I know about Paul, but who are you?' " Then the wild man leaped on them, tore their clothes off, and gave them such a beating that they fled in terror, "naked and bleeding."

Those seven brothers learned a lesson that day that I am sure they never forgot. Never again did they use the precious name of Jesus in a joking way or as if it were a conjurer's magic word.

SEVEN FOOLISH BROTHERS

There is power in the name of Jesus. But that power is revealed only when His name is used reverently and sincerely by one who loves the Lord with a devoted heart.

The devil feared Jesus and Paul, but he wasn't the least bit afraid of the seven sons of Sceva. They had no Christian experience. No power from heaven was flowing through their lives. They were just seven foolish young men playing with religion.

That makes me think. Is the devil afraid of me? Is he afraid of you?

Bonfire in Ephesus

(Acts 19:17-20:1)

WHENEVER someone is a bold witness for Jesus, you may be sure it won't be long before Satan stages a counterattack.

That's what happened in Ephesus. Paul's witness there was greatly blessed. Hundreds accepted Jesus. When they did, they threw away their idols and gave up all the worldly pleasures that were such a waste of their time and money.

The Bible says that "a number who had practiced sorcery brought their scrolls together and burned them publicly. When they calculated the value of the scrolls, the total came to fifty thousand drachmas [silver coins, each worth a day's wage]. In this way the word of the Lord spread widely and grew in power."

What a bonfire that must have been!

Seeing his own books burned was more than the devil could take. So he got a man named Demetrius to cause trouble for Paul and the new Christians.

This man was a silversmith, whose chief source of income came from making silver shrines for Artemis—the famous goddess of Ephesus. Gradually it dawned on him that if Paul's teachings spread much farther, there wouldn't be anybody left to buy his little silver shrines and idols.

He called a meeting of fellow silversmiths and said to them, "Men, you know we receive a good income from this business. And you see and hear how this fellow Paul has convinced and led astray large numbers of people here in Ephesus and in practically the whole province of Asia. He says that man-made gods are no gods at all. There is danger not only that our trade will lose its good name, but also that the temple of the great goddess Artemis will be discredited, and the goddess herself, who is worshiped throughout the province of Asia and the world, will be robbed of her divine majesty."

Demetrius put a lot of fire into his speech, and by the time he had finished, his friends were all stirred up. "Great is Artemis of the Ephesians!" they cried. "Great is Artemis of the Ephesians!"

Pretty soon they were running through the city, shouting this slogan until "the whole city was in an uproar." Grabbing two of Paul's companions, they rushed with them into the great open-air theater.

When he heard what had happened, Paul wanted to go

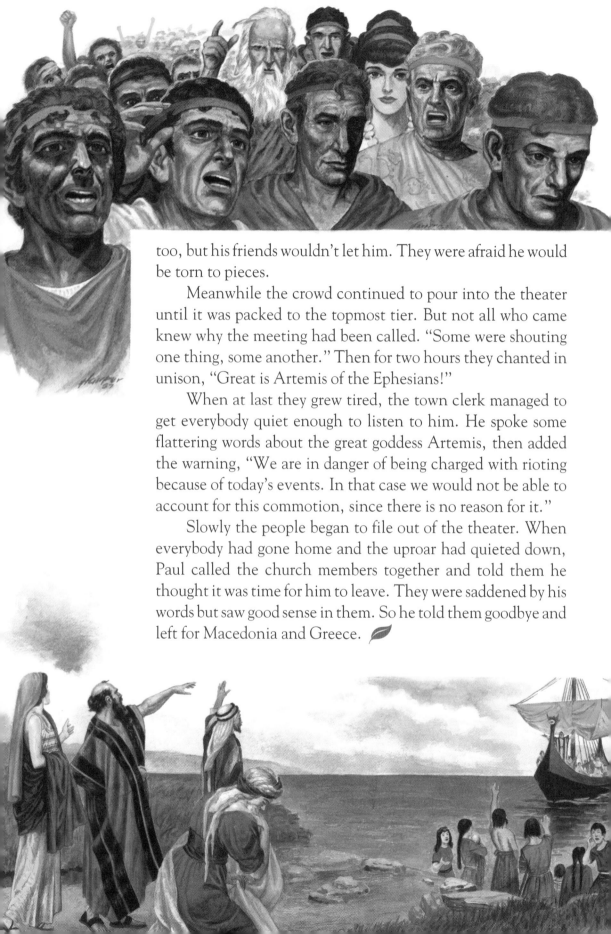

too, but his friends wouldn't let him. They were afraid he would be torn to pieces.

Meanwhile the crowd continued to pour into the theater until it was packed to the topmost tier. But not all who came knew why the meeting had been called. "Some were shouting one thing, some another." Then for two hours they chanted in unison, "Great is Artemis of the Ephesians!"

When at last they grew tired, the town clerk managed to get everybody quiet enough to listen to him. He spoke some flattering words about the great goddess Artemis, then added the warning, "We are in danger of being charged with rioting because of today's events. In that case we would not be able to account for this commotion, since there is no reason for it."

Slowly the people began to file out of the theater. When everybody had gone home and the uproar had quieted down, Paul called the church members together and told them he thought it was time for him to leave. They were saddened by his words but saw good sense in them. So he told them goodbye and left for Macedonia and Greece.

The Young Man
Who Slept in Church

(Acts 20:6-12)

IT HAPPENED at a place called Troas on the coast of Asia Minor. Paul had just returned from Greece, where he had gone to encourage the new believers.

After spending a week with the Christians in Troas, he had met with them again on the first day of the week in a room on the third story of a local building.

The grand old missionary had no doubt already preached in the morning and perhaps again Sabbath afternoon. Then, "on the first day of the week" which, in those days, began at sunset Saturday night, he held yet another meeting. He wanted to celebrate the Lord's Supper before leaving in the morning.

Nobody knows the exact hour when this meeting began, but we do know when it was interrupted and when it finally ended.

Paul had so much to say and so many wonderful stories to tell that he "kept on talking until midnight." How many people dozed during that long, long service we are not told, but the

name of the young man who went fast asleep will never be forgotten.

Eutychus was sitting in the window, and "was sinking into a deep sleep as Paul talked on and on." Evidently the window was open, for the poor lad fell out and hit the ground with a dreadful thud three stories down.

You can imagine the commotion. Paul was forgotten. Women screamed, and men rushed outside to see what had happened.

Everybody was wide awake now as the word was passed from one to another, "Eutychus fell out of the window, and he's dead."

A lantern held high in someone's hand showed where the body lay, and a crowd quickly gathered around it. Nobody could see much in the dim light.

Then Paul came striding through. Pressing his way to the front, he knelt down beside Eutychus and put his arms around him, much as Elisha, many years before, had held the dead son of the Shunammite woman.

After a few moments he stood up again. "Don't worry," he said. "He's alive."

Everybody was amazed. They couldn't understand it. But

there was no doubt that what Paul said was true.

After the meeting "the people took the young man home alive and were greatly comforted."

You might think that this would have brought the meeting to a close. Oh, no! After a little break Paul went right back to the pulpit and carried on from where he had left off. The Bible says that when he went upstairs again, he "broke bread and ate. After talking until daylight, he left."

What happened to Eutychus afterward we are not told. But when he heard his friends talking about that wonderful night when the apostle Paul preached in his church, he must always have had a feeling of regret. That was the greatest night in the history of Troas, and he had slept through much of it. It doesn't pay to sleep in church.

Sermon on the Stairs

(Acts 20:13-22:29)

WHAT energy and stamina the apostle Paul had! After preaching all night, he set out at daybreak by foot for Assos, 20 miles (32 kilometers) away. His friends, who had sailed around the peninsula by ship, planned to pick him up there. That was quite a walk for a Sunday morning!

When he arrived at Assos, the ship was waiting for him. It was a small vessel, which put in at various seaside cities along the coast of Asia Minor. When Paul reached Miletus, he sent a messenger to Ephesus, asking the elders of the church there to come and see him.

Feeling sure that he would never pass this way again, Paul gave them lots of good advice, entrusting them "to God and to the word of His grace."

"When he had said this, he knelt down with all of them and prayed." And the record says, "They all wept as they embraced him and kissed him. What grieved them most was his statement that they would never see his face again."

106

SERMON ON THE STAIRS

As the ship sailed out of the harbor, Paul stood on the deck, waving a last farewell to his friends on the shore. I am sure there were tears running down his cheeks as he called to them, "Goodbye, goodbye, God bless you!"

Then the wind caught the sails, and the ship rounded the point and was gone.

Some days later the party arrived at Tyre and spent a week with the church there. When it came time to leave, every member, including the wives and children, came to see them off. Kneeling on the beach, they prayed together and said goodbye to each other. It must have been a very touching sight, especially when Paul shook hands with the boys and girls. I can see them looking up at him with tear-dimmed eyes, so sad to think he would never come back again.

From Tyre it was just a short trip to Caesarea, where Paul and his friends went ashore. They stayed there for some time, and then went on to Jerusalem, where the church leaders gave them a warm welcome. Then Paul "reported in detail what God had done among the Gentiles through his ministry."

It was a great story, and "when they heard this, they praised God."

Then Paul went to the Temple. He was glad to see the familiar old building again after all his travels. And it was good to walk among the crowds that had flocked into the Temple court for the feast of Pentecost. How he wished these thousands would all accept Jesus as their Saviour! It was sad to think that 25 years after the Holy Spirit had come to the disciples in this very city, so many people still refused to listen to the gospel.

Suddenly he was recognized by some Jews who had stirred up hatred against him in the cities of Asia Minor. At once there was trouble.

"Men of Israel, help us!" they cried. "This is the man who teaches all men everywhere against our people and our law and this place. And besides, he has brought Greeks into the temple area and defiled this holy place."

The charge wasn't true, but it was enough to start a riot. Paul was seized and dragged out of the Temple court, and the gates were shut. Outside, more and more people came together, all shouting abuse at him and trying to hit him.

Paul would have been killed then and there, but the commander of the Roman troops suddenly appeared on the

108

scene with some officers and soldiers, and brought about order in the mob.

"What's going on here?" asked the commander. "Why are you beating this man?"

"Some . . . shouted one thing, some another," and the commander, thinking Paul must be some terrible criminal, ordered that he be put in chains and taken to the barracks.

On the way Paul spoke to the commander and tried to clear things up.

"Aren't you the leader of a band of terrorists?" asked the commander.

"No, indeed!" Paul assured him. "I am a Jew, from Tarsus in Cilicia, a citizen of no ordinary city. Please let me speak to the people."

Impressed by Paul's cultured speech and manner, the commander agreed. Standing on the stairs leading up to the barracks, Paul "motioned to the crowd." Astonished at the turn of events, they became quiet, wondering what this chained pris-

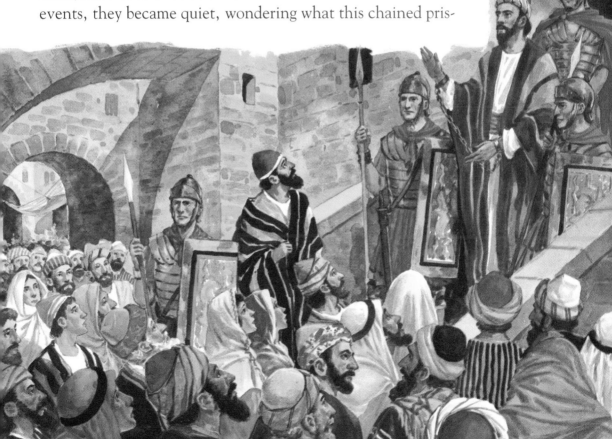

oner would have to say.

"Brothers and fathers," he cried in the language of the people, "listen now to my defense." Then he went on to tell his life story from his birth to his conversion on the Damascus road. The crowd listened intently until he said that the Lord had told him to go and preach to the Gentiles.

This was too much for his listeners. "Rid the earth of him! He's not fit to live!" they yelled, throwing off their cloaks and throwing dust in the air.

They made such a big uproar that Paul's voice was completely drowned. Fearing worse trouble, the commander moved his men up the steps and into the barracks. Then he ordered Paul to be flogged.

"Is it legal for you to flog a Roman citizen who hasn't even been found guilty?" Paul asked the centurion who was about to beat him.

Going to the commander, the centurion said, "You'd better be careful, sir. This man is a Roman citizen."

Worried, the commander went to Paul. "Are you a Roman citizen?" he asked.

"Yes, I am," said Paul.

"I had to pay a big price for my citizenship," the officer said.

" 'But I was born a citizen,' Paul replied."

A few hours later his chains were removed.

Boy With a Secret

(Acts 22:30-23:31)

THE next day the commander ordered the chief priests and their council to meet and listen to Paul's defense. They agreed, and Paul was taken to the meeting, which proved to be a very stormy one.

Scarcely had the apostle begun to speak when "a dispute broke out." Some took his part, others opposed him. The room was filled with angry shouts. "The commander was afraid Paul would be torn to pieces by them. He ordered the troops to go down and take him away from them by force and bring him into the barracks."

So the Romans saved Paul's life again. But the apostle was discouraged. He had been given a wonderful opportunity to witness before the Jewish leaders, and it seemed as if he had spoiled it. But Jesus knew he had done his best, and the next night, "the Lord stood near Paul and said, 'Take courage! As you have testified about me in Jerusalem, so you must also testify in Rome.' "

This cheered his heart, for he had always wanted to see

Rome, and now he knew that his life would be spared until this dream came true.

A short time later a boy knocked on the door of the barracks and asked permission to see Paul. "He's my uncle," he said, "and I have a message for him." The boy proved to be Paul's sister's son.

"What news do you bring me?" asked Paul.

Excitedly the boy told his story. He had learned of a plot that had been laid to take his uncle's life. More than 40 men had sworn not to eat or drink until they had killed him. They had asked the chief priests to request that the commander bring Paul to the council again. They planned to murder him on the way.

"Very interesting," I can hear Paul saying. "Thank you. Would you please tell this to the commander?"

"Certainly," said the boy, anxious to save his uncle's life.

The commander believed his story. After telling the boy to keep his secret well, he ordered two of his centurions to get ready "two hundred soldiers, seventy horsemen and two hundred spearmen" to take Paul to Caesarea and deliver him to Governor Felix.

That was quite a lot of men to look after one Christian preacher, but the commander was determined that no harm should come to Paul while the prisoner was in his custody.

After dark that night the soldiers began their journey. As they clattered out of the gates of Jerusalem, nobody dreamed that the cloaked figure on horseback in the middle was the apostle Paul. Nobody, that is, except Paul's nephew. I think he must have guessed. And I am sure he chuckled as he thought of those 40 men who had sworn to kill Paul. If they kept their oath, they would go hungry for a long, long time.

Heaven Missed by Inches

(*Acts 23:33-26:32*)

JESUS told His disciples that they would "be brought before governors and kings" * for His sake, and this certainly came true in the life of the apostle Paul.

Shortly after arriving in Caesarea he was brought before Governor Felix. Felix knew a good deal about the Christian faith, and he and his wife, Drusilla, had many talks with him. Once, as Paul spoke about "righteousness, self-control and the judgment to come," Felix became alarmed and said, "That's enough for now! You may leave. When I find it convenient, I will send for you."

At that moment Felix was very close to accepting Jesus as his Saviour, but he put off his decision to "when I find it convenient"—which never came. How near he was to the kingdom! How sad that he drew back! So near and yet so far!

After two years Felix was transferred to another post. In order "to grant a favor to the Jews, he left Paul in prison."

Festus, the new governor, ordered Paul to be brought before him so that he could find out for himself why this man had been kept in prison so long. He too treated Paul kindly, asking him whether he would like to go to Jerusalem for his trial.

Paul said No. "I am now standing before Caesar's court, where I ought to be tried. I have not done any wrong to the Jews, as you yourself know very well. If, however, I am guilty of doing anything deserving death, I do not refuse to die. But if the charges brought against me by these Jews are not true, no one has the right to hand me over to them. I appeal to Caesar!"

Festus turned to his councilors and asked for their advice. Then he said to Paul, "You have appealed to Caesar. To Caesar you will go!"

Before Paul could be sent to Rome, however, King Agrippa and his wife, Bernice, arrived in Caesarea. Festus told them about the famous prisoner he had on his hands, and the king said he would like to see him.

So a meeting was arranged. When Paul was brought in, King Agrippa told him to go ahead and tell him everything that was on his heart. Paul was delighted to have this chance. Once

again he told the story of his life and how Jesus had spoken to him on the Damascus road.

Then he related how, in obedience to this heavenly vision, he had gone everywhere, declaring that all men, both Jews and Gentiles, "should repent and turn to God and prove their repentance by their deeds."

As he explained how Christ fulfilled the Old Testament prophecies about the Messiah, he became so earnest that Festus suddenly interrupted him. " 'You are out of your mind, Paul!' he shouted. 'Your great learning is driving you insane.'

" 'I am not insane, most excellent Festus,' Paul replied. 'What I am saying is true and reasonable.' " Then, turning to the king he asked, "King Agrippa, do you believe the prophets? I know you do."

"Do you think that in such a short time you can persuade me to be a Christian?" asked the king.

"Short time or long—I pray God that not only you but all who are listening to me today may become what I am, except for these chains."

As the meeting came to a close King Agrippa told Festus, "This man could have been set free if he had not appealed to Caesar."

That was a great moment in the king's life. He was almost persuaded, but not quite. Like Felix, he put off deciding for Christ until another time, and put it off too long.

Like Felix, he almost stepped into heaven, only to lose it forever. He missed it by inches, as one might say. Let us be careful not to do the same thing ourselves. 🖋

---

* Matthew 10:18.

Chained to his captor, Paul told the story of his conversion to Christ with such courage and earnestness that King Agrippa was deeply moved and almost persuaded to believe.

Angel in the Storm

(Acts 27:1-28:31)

S INCE there was no ship sailing directly from Caesarea to Rome, Paul and some other prisoners were put on board a vessel bound for ports along the coast of Asia Minor. When this ship had gone as far as Myra, all the prisoners were transferred to another ship going to Italy.

What a voyage that was! Trouble began soon after they left port. The winds were unfavorable, and the ship traveled slowly, losing valuable days. By the time it reached Crete, it was nearly winter , so Paul advised the centurion to anchor there and wait for better weather. "But the centurion, instead of listening to what Paul said, followed the advice of the pilot." This was natural, and it was decided to sail on.

The pilot was soon sorry, for a gale sprang up, and he could do nothing but let the ship run before it. The next day the storm became worse, and the pilot decided to lighten the ship by throwing much of the cargo overboard. The day after that the tackle was thrown over, too.

"When neither sun nor stars appeared for many days and

the storm continued raging," all hope of being saved faded away. By this time most of the prisoners and crew were worn out with hunger, weariness, seasickness, and fear. Many were lying in the filthy hold, helpless, hopeless, and terrified.

Then Paul stood up, his face alight with courage and hope. As the ship rolled and tossed about in the mountainous seas, he somehow managed to keep his footing. "Men," he said, "you

should have taken my advice not to sail from Crete; then you would have spared yourselves this damage and loss. But now I urge you to keep up your courage, because not one of you will be lost; only the ship will be destroyed. Last night an angel of the God whose I am and whom I serve stood beside me and said, 'Do not be afraid, Paul. You must stand trial before Caesar; and God has graciously given you the lives of all who sail with you.' "

So God had heard Paul's prayers for his fellow prisoners and for the crew, for the pilot and the centurion.

And best of all, God had sent him a personal message of

comfort, and the angel carrying it had found his way through the dreadful storm, right into the hold of that sea-tossed vessel! How carefully God watches over His faithful children!

No wonder Paul's heart was full of courage! No wonder he could say to those poor, miserable soldiers and sailors, "So keep up your courage, men, for I have faith in God that it will happen just as he told me!"

And it did turn out exactly as he had said.

A few days later the ship ran aground on the island of Malta and was broken to pieces by the heavy seas.

The soldiers wanted to kill the prisoners so no one could escape, "but the centurion wanted to spare Paul's life and kept them from carrying out their plan. He ordered those who could swim to jump overboard first and get to land. The rest were to get there on planks or on pieces of the ship. In this way every-one reached land in safety."

There were 276 people on that ship and everyone was saved, just as Paul had promised.

Right after landing, as Paul was sitting by a fire trying to dry his clothes, a snake struck him and fastened itself on his hand. Those who saw this happen expected him to fall dead

at once, but instead he calmly shook off the creature and showed no effects of being bitten.

The natives were so astonished that they felt sure he must be some god. But he told them no, he was only a servant of the God of heaven. He went on to prove it by kind words and deeds.

After he had healed the father of the chief official of the island, "the rest of the sick on the island came and were cured." Heaven came close to Malta because of Paul's presence, and when the time came for Paul to leave, everybody was sad to see him go.

After three months on the island, the party set sail once more and finally reached Italy. To Paul's surprise, a few Christians came to meet him, and he "thanked God and was encouraged." When he arrived in Rome, although he was chained, he invited the local Jews to visit him. Many of them came, and he preached to them about Jesus.

What a man! The Bible says that for two years he preached and taught like this, "boldly and without hindrance." So he waited for his appointment to see Caesar, and for the martyr's death that lay ahead.

PART THREE

Stories of
the First
Christian
Letters

(Romans 1:1-Jude 25)

Paul's Love Letters

WHILE Paul was a prisoner in Rome he preached to his visitors but he also found time to write letters to the churches he had founded in Macedonia and Asia Minor.

Just how many letters Paul wrote while on his missionary journeys and while in prison, nobody knows. But he must have written far more than the dozen or so that exist today.

He is one of the most famous letter writers of all time. Some of his letters are still read every day by millions of people all around the world.

Half of the books of the New Testament were written by him. These "books" are really letters, or "epistles," as they are sometimes called. Some were addressed to churches in cities such as Corinth, Philippi, or Colossae. Others were written to personal friends like Timothy and Titus.

All of Paul's letters were love letters. You can't read them without feeling the love he had for the people to whom he wrote. He counted them all as his own sons and daughters. He

125

← PAINTING BY JES SCHLAIKJER, N.A.

After his eventful missionary journeys Paul was imprisoned in a Roman dungeon, but before he was put to death he wrote letters of encouragement to the churches he had served.

had suffered a lot in order to bring them the gospel, and they were all very dear to his heart. "You are our glory and joy" [1] he told them, and he meant every word.

Because he loved these new converts so much he sent them good advice on all sorts of subjects. He didn't want them to miss any spiritual gift as they waited for the return of Jesus.

He wanted to make sure that they would stay in the church and not be led away by false teachers. That is why he tried to make the gospel as plain to them as he could. Over and over again he told them just how God wanted them to act as Christians. Repeatedly he assured them that God by His Holy Spirit would give them power to live noble lives, such as God's children should lead.

Faithfully he warned them that their decision to be followers of Jesus would bring them trouble. Enemies would try to harm them. But they were not to worry. Earlier he had written these brave and encouraging words to the Romans: "Who shall separate us from the love of Christ? Shall trouble or hardship or persecution or famine or nakedness or danger or sword? As it is written: 'For your sake we face death all day long; we are considered as sheep to be slaughtered.' No, in all these things we are more than conquerors through him who loved us. For I am convinced that neither death nor life, neither angels nor demons, neither the present nor the future, nor any powers, neither height nor depth, nor anything else in all creation, will be able to separate us from the love of God that is in Christ Jesus our Lord." [2]

As you read Paul's love letters you will come across some things that may seem difficult to understand at first. Don't let

126

this worry you too much. Peter felt the same way about them, for he wrote: "His letters contain some things that are hard to understand." [3]

Always try to remember when these letters were written and to whom they were written. They are the oldest Christian letters in existence. They were written between A.D. 50 and 65—not many years after the crucifixion of Christ and only a little while after the new Christians had come out of pagan idolatry or from among the Jews. There was so much truth these dear people needed to know that it took someone with Paul's keen mind and loving heart to explain it all to them.

By studying Paul's letters to the Romans, Corinthians, Thessalonians, and the other epistles, you will learn about the Christian church as it was more than 1,900 years ago, and of the love in the heart of the man who did so much to raise it up.

---

[1] 1 Thessalonians 2:20.
[2] Romans 8:35-39.
[3] 2 Peter 3:16.

Love at Its Best

(1 Corinthians 13:1-14:1)

HAVE you ever asked yourself what is the meaning of the word "love"?

When you say, "I love my dog," or "I love my pet canary," or "I love my mother," what do you have in mind? Do you mean that you just have a nice friendly feeling inside you toward your dog, your canary, or your mother? Or is love something more than that?

It is really quite important that we know what love is, because it is the most important word in the Bible. "God is love" [1] we are told, and Jesus came from heaven to earth to explain this. When a lawyer asked Him, "Which is the greatest commandment in the law?" Jesus replied, " '*Love* the Lord your God with all your heart and with all your soul and with all your mind.' This is the first and greatest commandment. And the second is like it: '*Love* your neighbor as yourself.' " [2]

Jesus told His disciples, "My commandment is this: Love each other as I have loved you." [3]

It is plain that if we are going to be true followers of Jesus, we must learn to love and love and keep on loving. But how?

Paul tried to answer this question in his first letter to the church in Corinth. There had been trouble among the members. Some had been jealous. Others had been proud and boastful. All these feelings were wrong, he said, because they were the opposite of love.

"If I speak in the tongues of men and of angels," he said, "but have not love, I am only a resounding gong or a clanging cymbal.

"If I have the gift of prophecy and can fathom all mysteries and all knowledge, and if I have a faith that can move mountains, but have not love, I am nothing.

"If I give all I possess to the poor and surrender my body to the flames, but have not love, I gain nothing."

Then he went on to describe love and tell what it is and how it shows itself. "Love is patient, love is kind," he said. "It does not envy, it does not boast, it is not proud.

ABLE TO SPEAK MANY LANGUAGES — LOVE = O

ABLE TO SPEAK LIKE ANGELS — LOVE = O

ABLE TO PROPHESY — LOVE = O

ABLE TO UNDERSTAND MYSTERIES — LOVE = O

ABLE TO KNOW EVERYTHING — LOVE = O

FAITH TO REMOVE MOUNTAINS — LOVE = O

"It is not rude, it is not self-seeking, it is not easily angered, it keeps no record of wrongs.

"Love does not delight in evil but rejoices with the truth.

"It always protects, always trusts, always hopes, always perseveres.

"Love never fails. But where there are prophecies, they will cease; where there are tongues, they will be stilled; where there is knowledge, it will pass away. . . .

"And now these three remain: faith, hope and love. But the greatest of these is love." Then he added, "Follow the way of love."

Love is a good way for you and me to follow. We should try to reveal the love of God in our lives at all times and in all places—at home, at school, at work, at play.

Not just silly sentiment, but love, true love. Love that is patient and kind. Love that keeps us from being jealous, or boastful, or proud, or rude. Love that never lets us insist on our own way or be irritable or resentful. Love that rejoices in what is good but never in what is evil. Love believes the best about others and is always full of hope.

This is love at its best, said Paul. It is the kind of love that Christians should have in their hearts and reveal in their lives every day.

---
[1] 1 John 4:8.
[2] Matthew 22:36-39.
[3] John 15:12.

One Loving Family

(Galatians 2:16-6:2)

PAUL carried in his heart a beautiful picture of what the church should be. He saw it as one loving family in Christ.

If there was one thing he couldn't stand, it was the suggestion that there could be divisions in the church, such as Jewish Christians and Gentile Christians. This idea was quite wrong, he said. Those who accepted the gospel couldn't be separated. They all belonged together.

When the news reached him that the churches in Galatia were becoming divided over whether it was necessary to keep all the laws of Moses in order to be saved, he wrote them one of his strongest letters. "By observing the law no one will be justified," he said. "You are all sons of God through faith in Christ Jesus, for all of you who were baptized into Christ have clothed yourselves with Christ. There is neither Jew nor Greek, slave nor free, male nor female, for *you are all one in Christ Jesus.* If you belong to Christ, then you are Abraham's seed, and heirs according to the promise."

132

There was something far more important, he said, than trying to keep each law, and that was love. "The entire law is summed up in a single command: 'Love your neighbor as yourself.' "

Here he was back on his main theme again—love. It is love that matters most to God. Love alone will bring peace and harmony into the church.

If they opened their hearts to the Holy Spirit, they wouldn't have to worry about breaking any laws. Love would keep them doing right. Love would stop them from devouring one another in quarrels. It would stop them from doing everything unkind or hateful. For "the fruit of the Spirit is love," he said—"love, joy, peace, patience, kindness, goodness, faithfulness, gentleness and self-control. Against such things there is no law."

"Since we live by the Spirit," he added, "let us keep in step

with the Spirit. Let us not become conceited, provoking and envying each other. . . . Carry each other's burdens, and in this way you will fulfill the law of Christ."

This was good advice, not only for the Galatian churches but for us. Here is the secret of unity, of getting along together, and it will work in church, or school, or home. It is as simple as ABC. We don't need to try keeping a lot of rules and regulations. We just need to say earnestly to God, "Please fill my heart with Your Holy Spirit." For God is love, and His Spirit is the Spirit of love. And when He comes in, everything unlovely goes out.

This is the way—the only way—by which fathers and mothers, boys and girls, of all nations and tongues and peoples can become one loving family in Christ. It is the way to peace, friendliness, and happiness today, tomorrow, always. Why don't we follow it?

God's Armor

(Ephesians)

W HEN Paul wrote from Rome to his old friends in
Ephesus, he reminded them that they too were
part of one loving family in Christ.

To those who had come into the church from pagan
idolatry he said, "Remember that formerly you who are Gentiles . . . were separate from Christ, excluded from citizenship
in Israel and foreigners to the covenants of the promise,
without hope and without God in the world. But now in
Christ Jesus you who once were far away have been brought
near through the blood of Christ. For he himself is our peace,
who *has made the two one* and has destroyed the barrier, the
dividing wall of hostility."

That is what the gospel does. It brings strangers together. It
breaks down dividing walls.

"Consequently," Paul went on, "you are no longer foreigners and aliens, but fellow citizens with God's people and members of God's household."

He prayed a beautiful prayer for this loving, united family,

that they might go on learning more and more about God's love. "I kneel before the Father, from whom his whole family in heaven and on earth derives its name. I pray that out of his glorious riches he may strengthen you with power through his Spirit in your inner being, so that Christ may dwell in your hearts through faith.

"And I pray that you, being rooted and established in love, may have power, together with all the saints, to grasp how wide and long and high and deep is the love of Christ, and to *know this love* that surpasses knowledge—that you may be filled to the measure of all the fullness of God."

He begged them "to live a life worthy of the calling you have received. Be completely humble and gentle; be patient, bearing with one another in love. Make every effort to keep the unity of the Spirit through the bond of peace."

"Live a life of love," he urged, "just as Christ loved us and gave himself up for us as a fragrant offering and sacrifice to God."

"Put on the full armor of God," he said to them, "so that you can take your stand against the devil's schemes."

Paul did not mean that God wore armor like the Roman soldiers they saw every day. No, His armor is not made of anything material. It is made of truth, righteousness, and love. This is the armor every Christian must wear if he is to be victorious in all the battles of life.

"Stand firm then," said Paul, "with the belt of truth buckled around your waist, with the breastplate of righ-

137

Wearing the helmet of salvation, the strong shield of faith, and the sharp sword of the Spirit, the Christian warrior is able to withstand all the fiery assaults of Satan.

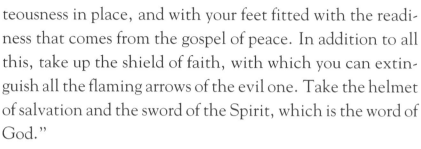

teousness in place, and with your feet fitted with the readiness that comes from the gospel of peace. In addition to all this, take up the shield of faith, with which you can extinguish all the flaming arrows of the evil one. Take the helmet of salvation and the sword of the Spirit, which is the word of God."

Perhaps as Paul was writing these words, he looked up at the tall Roman soldier standing beside him, admiring his brass helmet, his steel breastplate, his leather boots, his sharp sword and gleaming shield. Then he thought of the humble Christians at Ephesus. He remembered the frightful time in the theater when for two hours the people shouted, "Great is Artemis of the Ephesians."

"God's people could use some armor like this Roman soldier is wearing," he thought. Yet, even more, they needed spiritual armor to help them resist all the temptations of the evil one and to keep their hearts pure, true, loyal, and full of hope and confidence in God.

To live a good life, the life of love, the life of the true follower of Jesus, you need to wrap yourself in truth and put on the breastplate of righteousness, the shoes of peace, and the helmet of salvation. Then, with the shield of faith in one hand and the sword of the Spirit in the other, you will be able to face the worst enemies unafraid. Covered with God's armor, you are bound to win.

Eyes on the Prize

(Philippians)

A S PAUL sat in his prison in Rome and recalled all the adventures he had had while preaching the gospel, he thought with special tenderness of the Christians in Philippi.

It was there that he had first seen the inside of a dungeon. He remembered the jailer who had washed his wounds and accepted Jesus the same night. He thought of Lydia, who had opened her home to him, and of the other women who had often met with him for prayer on the riverbank. What wonderful people! How he loved them!

"I thank my God every time I remember you," he told them in his letter. "In all my prayers for all of you, I always pray with joy because of your partnership in the gospel from the first day until now."

"I have you in my heart . . . ," he wrote. "God can testify how I long for all of you with the affection of Christ Jesus. And this is my prayer: that your love may abound more and more . . . , so that you may be able to discern what is best and may be

139

pure and blameless until the day of Christ."

Like his messages to the Galatians and the Ephesians, his letter to the Philippians was full of concern that they remain united in the faith. "Stand firm in one spirit, contending as one man for the faith of the gospel."

He urged them to be "like-minded, having the same love. . . . Do nothing out of selfish ambition or vain conceit," he said, "but in humility consider others better than yourselves." "Do everything without complaining or arguing, so that you may become blameless and pure, children of God without fault in a crooked and depraved generation, in which you shine like stars in the universe."

What a lovely word picture he painted of every member of the church—every man and woman, every boy and girl, letting his or her light shine, twinkling like a star on a dark night.

Then Paul went on to talk about himself and his hopes for the future. He had once held high office among the Jews. He had had money and possessions. "But whatever was to my profit," he wrote, "I now consider loss for the sake of Christ. What is more, I consider everything a loss compared to the surpassing greatness of knowing Christ Jesus my Lord, for whose sake I have lost all things.

"I consider them rubbish, that I may gain Christ and be found in him, not having a righteousness of my own that comes from the law, but . . . the righteousness that comes from God and is by faith. I want to know Christ and the power of his resurrection and the fellowship of sharing in his sufferings, . . . and so, somehow, to attain to the resurrection from the dead.

141

"Not that I have already . . . been made perfect," he added, "but I press on to take hold of that for which Christ Jesus took hold of me. . . . One thing I do: Forgetting what is behind and straining toward what is ahead, I press on toward the goal to win the prize for which God has called me heavenward in Christ Jesus."

He had his eyes on the prize that God has promised all who accept Jesus as their Saviour. He longed for the day of Christ's return, for the resurrection morning, and the joy of living forever with his beloved Lord. To him it was a prize worth everything it might cost in this life, and he wanted the Philippian believers to keep their eyes on it too.

"Therefore, my brothers, you whom I love and long for, my joy and crown," he said, "that is how you should stand firm in the Lord, dear friends! . . . Rejoice in the Lord always. I will say it again: Rejoice! . . . Do not be anxious about anything, but in everything, by prayer and petition, with thanksgiving, present your requests to God. And the peace of God, which transcends all understanding, will guard your hearts and your minds in Christ Jesus."

Paul's epistle to the Philippians was perhaps his most tender and beautiful love letter. Because he loved these people so much, he revealed to them the secret motives of his life, the glorious prize he kept fixed before his eyes.

It makes me wonder what prize you are attracted to. Is it money, or a big house, or lots of land, or an important job? Or, like Paul, have you decided that nothing the world has to offer can be compared with living forever with Jesus?

Love's Knitting

(Colossians)

WHEN Paul began to write to the new Christians in Colossae, he didn't get very far before he was back on the subject of love. To him nothing was more important than the love that the followers of Jesus should have for one another.

First, he told them how pleased he was to hear of their faith and love; but he went on to say that he wanted them to become more loving still. He said he prayed every day that they would "live a life worthy of the Lord and may please him in every way: bearing fruit in every good work, growing in the knowledge of God."

It was his special desire, he added, that their hearts would be *"united in love,"* or as the old King James Version puts it, "knit together in love."

The original word has the thought of *bringing together*. Close together, as when you knot two pieces of string, or knit two strands of yarn, or weld two pieces of iron.

And that's exactly what love does. It brings people together. Fathers and mothers, parents and children, brothers and sisters, new friends and old. And it does the best kind of uniting. People united by love stay together—always.

Further on in his letter to the Colossians, Paul came back to this same sweet thought. He urged them to get *rid* of such unlovely things as "anger, rage, malice, slander, and filthy language from your lips" and to *clothe* themselves with "compassion, kindness, humility, gentleness and patience. Bear with each other and forgive . . . one another."

Then he added, "And over all these virtues put on love, *which binds them all together in perfect unity*. Let the peace of Christ rule in your hearts. . . . And whatever you do, whether in word or deed, do it all in the name of the Lord Jesus, giving thanks to God the Father through him."

Here he was back to knitting again—the knitting power of the love of Christ.

If your home is not a happy place, if people are quarreling and saying unkind things to one another, you may be sure it is time for somebody to start knitting—not with needles and a ball of yarn, but with the tender, gracious, forgiving love of Jesus—and bring people together.

I hope you'll be the one to do it.

Comfort for the Sorrowful

(1 Thessalonians 3:12-4:17)

PAUL had the same concern for the believers in Thessalonica as he had for all the others he had brought out of heathenism and Judaism into the Christian church. He wanted them to have more and more love for others, until their hearts were full to overflowing with the love of God.

"May the Lord make your love increase and overflow for each other and for everyone else," he said to them. "May he strengthen your hearts so that you will be blameless and holy in the presence of our God and Father when our Lord Jesus comes with all his holy ones."

"You yourselves have been taught by God to love each other," he added. "And in fact, you do love all the brothers throughout Macedonia. Yet we urge you, brothers, *to do so more and more*."

He wanted them never to be satisfied until the love that shone out of their hearts was a perfect reflection of the love of God in Christ Jesus.

But he had a special message for these dear people. Some of them were sad and discouraged because their loved ones had died. They were lonely, and puzzled too, wondering why God had let this happen.

Tenderly, kindly, Paul tried to comfort them. "Brothers, we do not want you to be ignorant about those who fall asleep," he wrote, "or to grieve like the rest of men, who have no hope."

Their loved ones were just sleeping, waiting for Jesus to come and wake them up.

The good news, he went on, is "that Jesus died and rose again, and so we believe that God will take back with Jesus those who have died believing in him" (TEV).

"According to the Lord's own word," Paul continued, "we tell you that we who are still alive, who are left till the coming

PAINTING BY FRED COLLINS

of the Lord, will certainly not precede those who have fallen asleep."

In other words, one will not go ahead of another; we will all go home together.

"For the Lord himself will come down from heaven, with a loud command, with the voice of the archangel and with the trumpet call of God, and the dead in Christ will rise first. After that, we who are still alive and are left will be caught up together with them in the clouds to meet the Lord in the air. And so we will be with the Lord forever. Therefore encourage each other with these words."

There was no need for them to worry anymore. No need to be sad. For Jesus was coming again, and He would give life to the dead on the glad resurrection morning. Then they would be "caught up together" to meet the Lord in the air.

"Together." That is God's plan. To bring loved ones and friends together again and to let them be together forever and ever. No more parting, no more sorrow, no more tears.

What precious words! "Together." "With the Lord forever."

If you know a neighbor or a school friend who is sad and sorrowful, why not tell him about this blessed and beautiful hope?

Fight the Good Fight!

(1 Timothy and 2 Timothy)

A S YOU may remember, when Paul visited Lystra on his first missionary journey, the people had stoned him and left him out at the city dump, thinking he was dead. It was there that he brought a young man named Timothy to Christ, as well as his mother and grandmother.

Later Paul asked Timothy to be his secretary and to help in the work of spreading the gospel. Timothy agreed, and from then on a wonderful friendship developed between the two men. They traveled together and wrote together.

Paul loved Timothy as deeply as if he was his own son. When they were separated, he sent the young man some good advice to help him in his work and encourage him to always be loyal to God.

Two of Paul's letters to Timothy still exist. You should read them. They are not very long. Their age—over 1,900 years—makes them precious, but their greatest value lies in the good advice they contain, given by an old man to a

149

young man in the first century of the Christian Era.

"Train yourself to be godly," Paul wrote in his first letter. "For physical training is of some value, but godliness has value for all things, holding promise for both the present life and the life to come."

"Don't let anyone look down on you because you are young," he said, "but set an example for the believers in speech, in life, in love, in faith and in purity."

To warn young people against thinking of money as the most important aim in life, he told Timothy that "people who want to get rich fall into temptation and a trap and into many foolish and harmful desires that plunge men into ruin and destruction. For the love of money is a root of all kinds of evil. . . .

"But you, man of God, flee from all this, and pursue righteousness, godliness, faith, love, endurance and gentleness.

"*Fight the good fight* of the faith. Take hold of the eternal life."

The second letter was written shortly before Paul was put to death in Rome. But though he was about to be beheaded, the apostle was more concerned about Timothy than himself.

"Flee the evil desires of youth," he wrote, "and pursue righteousness, faith, love and peace, along with those who call on the Lord out of a pure heart.

"Don't have anything to do with foolish and stupid arguments, because you know they produce quarrels. And the

Lord's servant must not quarrel; instead, he must be kind to everyone, able to teach, not resentful. Those who oppose him he must gently instruct."

After reminding Timothy that his mother had taught him "the holy Scriptures" from his childhood, he said that these inspired Scriptures, if read and studied, would make the man of God "thoroughly equipped for every good work."

Then he gave the young man this solemn charge. "In the presence of God and of Christ Jesus, who will judge the living and the dead, and in view of his appearing and his kingdom, I give you this charge: *Preach the Word*; be prepared in season and out of season; correct, rebuke and encourage—with great patience and careful instruction. . . .

"But you, keep your head in all situations, endure hardship, do the work of an evangelist, discharge all the duties of your ministry."

Then he added this touching farewell. "I am already being poured out like a drink offering, and the time has come for my departure. *I have fought the good fight*, I have finished the race, I have kept the faith. Now there is in store for me the crown of righteousness, which the Lord, the righteous Judge, will award to me on that day—and not only to me, but also to all who have longed for his appearing."

Paul wanted Timothy to "fight the good fight" too. It was his earnest wish for every young man, every boy and girl, in the Christian church long ago. If he were here now, it would be his wish for you and me.

The Runaway Slave

(Titus and Philemon)

IN YOUR Bible, right after Paul's two letters to Timothy, you will find two even shorter letters. One is addressed to Titus, the other to Philemon.

The first of these is full of good advice to another young man who was helping to spread the gospel. "In everything set them an example by doing what is good," Paul wrote to him. "In your teaching show integrity, seriousness and soundness of speech that cannot be condemned."

Then he summarized the whole purpose of the Christian faith in these great words: "For the grace of God that brings salvation has appeared to all men. It teaches us to say 'No' to ungodliness and worldly passions, and to live self-controlled, upright and godly lives in this present age, while we wait for the blessed hope—the glorious appearing of our great God and Saviour, Jesus Christ, who gave himself for us to redeem us from all wickedness and to purify for himself a people that are his very own, eager to do what is good."

The blessed hope of *the church* is the return in glory of Jesus

152

PAINTING BY CHARLES ZINGARO →

Jesus said, "And I, if I be lifted up from the earth, will draw all men unto me," and countless millions from every walk of life have yielded to the appeal of His outstretched hands.

Christ. But the blessed hope *of God* is to gather out of the world "a people that are his very own," rescued from "all wickedness," pure, holy, beautiful, and "eager to do what is good."

Though Paul's little note to Philemon is not very long, it is one of the most exciting books of the Bible. It is all about a runaway slave.

Philemon was the slaveowner, and Onesimus the slave. Both had become Christians, but Christianity had not yet destroyed the old, hateful custom of slavery. The law allowed a Roman to buy as many slaves as he could afford. These poor slaves had little control over their own lives. If they tried to escape and were recaptured, their owners had the right to torture them or kill them as they pleased.

Paul was faced with a dilemma when he brought Onesimus to Christ and learned that he was a runaway slave. Spiritually Onesimus was free, but legally he was still the slave of Philemon, also a convert of Paul.

What should be done? Should Paul tell Onesimus to go on trying to hide from his master or send him back?

Paul decided to send him back, and Onesimus agreed to go. And that's what this brief "love letter" is all about. It is a model of tactfulness. Notice how graciously Paul approached the matter.

"I always thank my God as I remember you in my prayers, because I hear about your faith in the Lord Jesus and your love for all the saints. . . . Your love has given me great joy and encouragement, because you, brother, have refreshed the hearts of the saints."

It was love that was needed just now. Lots of love.

Ever so gently, he came to the point. "I appeal to you for my son Onesimus, who became my son while I was in chains. . . . I am sending him—who is my very heart—back to you. I would have liked to keep him with me. . . . But I did not want to do anything without your consent. . . .

"Perhaps the reason he was separated from you for a little while was that you might have him back for good—no longer as a slave, but better than a slave, as a dear brother. . . . So if you consider me a partner, welcome him as you would welcome me. If he has done you any wrong or owes you anything, charge it to me."

The Bible doesn't tell us what happened when Philemon received this beautiful letter. But the story has come down through the centuries that Onesimus was accepted as a brother and later became a leader in the church. And so the love of God in Christ won one of its earliest victories over the wicked custom of slavery.

Keep Up Your Courage!

(Hebrews)

THE LETTER to the Hebrews was written to certain Jews who had accepted Christ as their Saviour. Paul tried to strengthen the faith of these dear people and help them to keep up their courage.

"We must pay more careful attention, therefore, to what we have heard," he told them, "so that we do not drift away." "See to it, brothers," he warned, "that none of you has a sinful, unbelieving heart that turns away from the living God."

They needed to think more about Christ and His sufferings, and how He had been crowned "with glory and honor."

"Since we have a great high priest who has gone through the heavens, Jesus the Son of God, let us hold firmly to the faith we profess.

"For we do not have a high priest who is unable to sympathize with our weaknesses, but we have one who has been tempted in every way, just as we are—yet was without sin.

"Let us then approach the throne of grace with confidence, so that we may receive mercy and find grace to help us in our time of need."

157

Jesus often prayed to His Father in heaven in behalf of His disciples. How comforting it is to know that when we pray to God, Jesus intercedes in our behalf as our high priest.

Still worried about them, he urged, "Do not throw away your confidence; it will be richly rewarded. You need to persevere so that when you have done the will of God, you will receive what he has promised. For in just a very little while, 'He who is coming will come and will not delay.' "

To encourage them to hold on to the truth they had learned, he reminded them of the great heroes of the past who had stayed true to God no matter what it had cost them.

"By faith Abel" offered the right sacrifice, though it meant his death.

"By faith Enoch" walked with God in a very evil time.

"By faith Noah" built the ark when nobody had ever heard of rain.

"By faith Abraham" left his home not knowing where he was going. And he and Sarah had faith in God when He said she would have a baby in her old age.

"By faith Abraham" required to offer his only son Isaac as a sacrifice, obeyed without question the strange command, believing God could raise him from the dead.

ABEL

ENOCH

NOAH

SARAH

"By faith Isaac" asked future blessings on Jacob and Esau.

"By faith Jacob" blessed the sons of Joseph.

"By faith Moses' parents hid him" among the reeds after he was born.

"By faith Moses" chose to suffer with God's people "rather than to enjoy the pleasures of sin for a short time."

"By faith the people" of Israel crossed the Red Sea.

"By faith the prostitute Rahab" gave shelter to the spies in Jericho.

It was a long list, but not long enough.

"And what more shall I say?" asked the writer. "I do not have time to tell about Gideon, Barak, Samson, Jephthah, David, Samuel and the prophets, who through faith conquered kingdoms, administered justice, and gained what was promised; who shut the mouths of lions, quenched the fury of the flames, and escaped the edge of the sword; whose weakness was turned to strength; and who became powerful in battle and routed foreign armies. . . .

"Others were tortured. . . . Some faced jeers and flogging, while still others were chained and put in prison.

MOSES

**MOSES'
MOTHER**

ABRAHAM

JACOB

CROSSING RED SEA

RAHAB

GIDEON

DAVID

"They were stoned; they were sawed in two; they were put to death by the sword. They went about in sheepskins and goatskins, destitute, persecuted and mistreated—the world was not worthy of them. They wandered in deserts and mountains, and in caves and holes in the ground."

So he retold the moving story of the great heroes of faith. Then he made his point. With all these examples of loyalty, with "such a great cloud of witnesses" to think about, how dare anyone consider giving up the faith now?

Rather, he urged, "let us throw off everything that hinders and the sin that so easily entangles, and let us run with perseverance the race marked out for us. Let us fix our eyes on Jesus, the author and perfecter of our faith, who for the joy set before him endured the cross, scorning its shame, and sat down at the right hand of the throne of God."

Here is something for us to remember too. When we begin to feel discouraged, we should try to think of others who have suffered for their faith far more than we ever have. More important still, we should look to Jesus, who endured so much for us and is now seated at God's right hand, waiting to cheer us up.

Let us keep up our courage!

God Is Love

(James, 1 Peter, 2 Peter, and 1 John)

THE LAST seven books of the Bible—apart from the book of Revelation—are really six short letters. Two of them were written by Peter, three by John, and one by Christ's own brother James, and one by Jude, James's brother.

Some think this James was later the leader of the church council in Jerusalem, and his letter was full of good advice for the whole church. He told the people to be glad when they had trials, because trials would make them stronger Christians.

If they needed wisdom, they were to ask God for it. They were to be "quick to listen, slow to speak and slow to become angry." And they were to "look after orphans and widows" and to keep themselves "from being polluted by the world." This, he said, was pure religion.

Some of James's best advice was about the use of the tongue. He must have run into a lot of trouble from careless gossipers.

Horses have bits to guide them, he said, and ships have

rudders. "But no man can tame the tongue." It can set the world on fire, even as a small blaze can burn down a forest. Only God can keep it under control. And for this He must give "the wisdom that comes from heaven" which "is first of all pure; then peace-loving, considerate, submissive, full of mercy."

"Do not slander one another," "Don't grumble against each other." "Do not swear," said James. And the wisdom of God would prevent all these faults.

Perhaps you and I need more heavenly wisdom to keep our tongues from saying the wrong words!

Peter's two letters paint a picture of the kind, loving, gentle Saviour he had lived with for three and a half years.

They were redeemed, he wrote, "not with perishable things such as silver or gold . . . but with the precious blood of Christ, a lamb without blemish or defect." "Rid yourselves of all malice and all deceit, hypocrisy, envy, and slander of every kind."

Jesus, said Peter, set us an example of patience and gentleness. "When they hurled their insults at him, he did not

162

retaliate; when he suffered, he made no threats." So we should beautify ourselves with "the unfading beauty of a gentle and quiet spirit, which is of great worth in God's sight."

"Finally, all of you," he pleaded, "live in harmony with one another; be sympathetic, love as brothers, be compassionate and humble."

Because he was sure Christ would return in glory to clean the earth with fire, he asked, "What kind of people ought you to be? You ought to live holy and godly lives as you look forward to the day of God and speed its coming."

That is a good question for us to ask ourselves.

In his three letters, John describes the test of a true Christian. He said, "We know that we have passed from death to life, *because we love our brothers.*"

It is love that matters most to God—love shown by kind, friendly, compassionate deeds.

"Dear children," wrote John, "let us not love with words or tongue but with actions and in truth." "Dear friends," he went on, "let us love one another, for love comes from God. Everyone who loves has been born of God and knows God. Whoever does not love does not know God, because *God is love.*"

These three little words are the most wonderful in all the Holy Scriptures. Strangely, they do not appear until almost the very end of the Bible story. Yet in one form or another they have been there all the time—all the way from Genesis to John.

When Adam roamed the sinless earth, he must often have whispered to himself, "God is love."

163

When the ark rested on Mount Ararat, Noah may well have said to his family, "God is love."

When Moses took the tables of the law from God's hands on Sinai, he must have thought, "God is love."

When Israel entered the Promised Land, their grateful songs said, "God is love."

When they returned from captivity in Babylon, they cried again, "God is love."

When the prophets gave their appeals and warnings, they were really saying, "God is love."

When Jesus came to dwell among men, He declared by everything He said and did that God is love.

And when He hung upon the cross of Calvary, there was no longer any doubt that God is love.

The whole glorious plan of redemption is summed up in these three of the simplest yet greatest words in the English language: God is love.

PART FOUR

Stories of

Christ's Final Triumph

(Revelation 1:1-22:21)

The Voice Behind You

(Revelation 1:1-18)

OR THE first 50 or so years after the crucifixion of Jesus, the gospel of His love was carried far and wide by His faithful followers. Groups of Christians appeared in all the chief cities of the Roman Empire. Farther and farther the message spread until it had been preached "to every creature under heaven." [1]

But not everyone welcomed the good news of the gospel. Many people refused to accept Jesus as their Saviour. They didn't want Him to change their lives. They would not give up their evil habits. Angrily they turned against the Christians and hurt them in every way they could.

By the year A.D. 90 all the apostles except John had been put to death, and he was an exile on the island of Patmos in the eastern Mediterranean. Let us go back across the years and visit him there.

It is the Sabbath, "the Lord's day," and John is sitting on a rock, looking out across the wide blue sea. Not a bit like the young fisherman who once heard the call of Jesus by Galilee, he

167

← PAINTING BY JES. SCHLAIKJER, N.A.

In exile on Patmos, the beloved John was given a vision of the triumphs of the gospel message to that time when the New Jerusalem would come down from God out of heaven.

is now an old man with a wrinkled face, gray hair, and a long gray beard. Alone, separated from all his friends, he is silently thinking of the past.

What memories crowd his mind! That first moment he met Jesus! Those kind, gentle eyes of the Master! His soft, loving voice! His earnest invitation, "Follow Me!"

He recalls the years of sweet companionship. What a wonderful friend Jesus had been! He was the sweetest, noblest soul who ever lived. How tenderly He had ministered to the poor and needy! What joy and peace He had left in people's hearts wherever He went! It was hard to believe that some could have hated Him enough to crucify Him. Yet they had.

He remembers the trial of Jesus and the heartbreaking procession to Golgotha. The nails being driven through His hands and feet. His gracious words, "Father, forgive them, for they do not know what they are doing." [2] His kindness toward the repentant thief. His last thought for His mother. "Here is your mother!" [3] He had said, and John had cared for her the best he could until her death.

He pictures the Resurrection. What a day that was! Could he ever forget running to the tomb with Peter and finding it empty? Or that thrilling moment when Jesus appeared to the disciples, saying, "Peace be with you"? [4] That was when the glorious truth had dawned on him that Jesus had actually risen from the dead.

After that the Master had gone away to heaven. John can still picture Him rising higher and higher, farther and farther, until "a cloud hid him from their sight." [5] He can still feel the loss and loneliness that came over him at that moment, and the surge of hope as the two men in white brought the comforting tidings, "This same Jesus, who has been taken from you into heaven, will come back in the same way you have seen him go into heaven." [6]

Sixty years had passed since then. And still the Master had not returned. Why? Could He have forgotten?

"It is a pity He has stayed away so long," John says to himself. So many things have gone wrong. James has been killed. So has Peter—crucified upside down, some say. Paul has died too, beheaded outside the walls of Rome. All of the disciples except John are in their graves, and he is just one short step from his. Yet Jesus has not come back. There is no word, no sign from heaven. Nothing but silence. Sixty years of silence. Why? Why? Why? Was there a mistake?

Suddenly John hears "a loud voice like a trumpet." He looks around, startled.

And there, right behind him, he sees Jesus. John has no

doubt who He is. Though His head and hair are "white like wool, as white as snow," His eyes "like blazing fire," His feet "like bronze," and His voice "like the sound of rushing waters," yet it is the same dear face he knows so well.

Overjoyed, John falls at his Master's feet. Gently Jesus puts His hand on the old, bent head, saying, "Do not be afraid. I am the First and the Last. I am the Living One; I was dead, and behold I am alive for ever and ever! And I hold the keys of death and Hades."

It is as though He said, "John, you are not the last of those who founded My church. I am. And as long as I live My cause is not lost. Even though Peter and James and all the rest have died, and you may die, everything will be all right in the end.

"I have the keys of death. Someday I shall open the graves of all who believe in Me. I am Alpha and Omega, the first and the last. I was there at the beginning of the fight with evil. I shall be there at the end. I will be alive forever. The final victory will be mine. Hold on to your faith. I will not fail you."

If you ever feel sad and discouraged, if you ever think you are the only one left who stands for right and truth, listen, like John, for the voice behind you. Jesus is never far away, and His voice, like the voice of a trumpet, will give you courage to go on.

---

[1] Colossians 1:23.   [3] John 19:27.   [5] Acts 1:9.
[2] Luke 23:34.   [4] John 20:19.   [6] Acts 1:11.

Overcomers for Christ

(Revelation 1:19-3:22)

CHRIST did not appear on Patmos just to comfort His faithful old follower John. He had a message for His church, and He knew that John was the best one to pass it on.

"Write what you see in a book," He said, "and send it to the seven churches, to Ephesus and to Smyrna and to Pergamum and to Thyatira and to Sardis and to Philadelphia and to Laodicea."

These were the names of seven cities of those days in which the Christian faith had taken root. Each had its group of believers who were witnessing for Christ.

All of these groups, or churches, were dear to the Master. He described them as "lampstands" shining brightly in the darkness of paganism. He was their Lord, always walking among them, watching with deep concern everything they did and everything that happened to them.

He was worried about some of them. Their lights were not as bright as they should be. Some members had lost their first

love. Others were allowing worldliness to come into their hearts. So He sent them words of rebuke and warning, at the same time encouraging them to do right, with promises of rich rewards for faithfulness.

He offered seven wonderful blessings to those who would overcome all evil and conquer all temptation.

To the members in Ephesus He said, "To him who overcomes, I will give the right to eat from the tree of life, which

172

is in the paradise of God."

He wanted them to remember that, however much they might suffer for Him in this life, they would be abundantly repaid in the life to come. Paradise, beautiful Eden, would be their home, and the fruit of the tree of life would be their food, through all eternity.

To the persecuted Christians of Smyrna He said, "Be faithful, even to the point of death, and I will give you the crown of life. . . . He who overcomes will not be hurt at all by the second death."

If they were killed because of their witness for Him, He would be sure to raise them up at

PAINTING BY WILLIAM HUTCHINSON

the first resurrection, never to die again.

To the church in Pergamum He said, "To him who overcomes, I will give some of the hidden manna. I will also give him a white stone with a new name written on it, known only to him who receives it."

In the Most Holy Place of the desert tabernacle was a jar of manna, a symbol of the spiritual food God provides for His people. The faithful in Pergamum would have all of this food

173

they needed. The gift of a white stone is part of a beautiful old custom in which the giver pledges friendship and hospitality. So the Christian overcomer may be certain of the eternal friendship and hospitality of Christ.

Thyatira was given this promise: "To him who overcomes and does my will to the end, I will give authority over the nations. . . . I will also give him the morning star."

The faithful could be sure that they would share Christ's final victory. If they suffered *for* Him, they would reign *with* Him. And they would possess the Morning Star, which is Christ Himself.

To Sardis He said, "He who overcomes will . . . be dressed in white. I will never blot out his name from the book of life, but will acknowledge his name before my Father and his angels."

This was another glorious promise of future victory and eternal reward. Not only would the faithful ones have their names kept forever in the book of life but Christ would talk about their loyalty right in the presence of the Father and the angels. They would be sure to have a royal welcome into the courts of glory.

Overcomers in the Philadelphia church were told: "Him who overcomes I will make a pillar in the temple of my God. Never again will he leave it. I will write on him the name of my

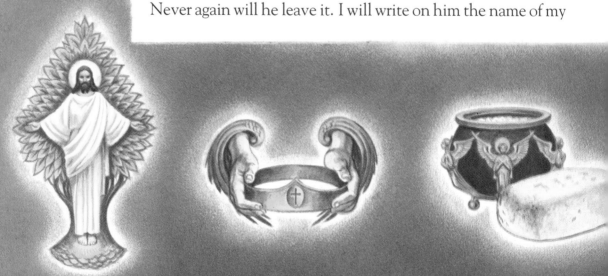

God and the name of the city of my God, the new Jerusalem. . . . I will also write on him my new name."

This was a marvelous promise of everlasting fellowship with God. The conquering Christian will have God's name written on him as well as the name and address of his heavenly home. It will be clear to everyone that he belongs to God and that His home is the New Jerusalem. He will be like a letter marked "Heaven—Special Delivery," and God will see that he gets there.

Finally, the members in Laodicea were told: "To him who overcomes, I will give the right to sit with me on my throne."

It was as if Christ had said, "The best of everything I have shall be yours." It meant that there was no limit to what He was willing to do for those who were true and faithful to Him. What more could He offer them?

These wonderful promises were not, of course, only for the members of these seven churches in Asia Minor. They are for Christian overcomers everywhere, in every age. They are for grownups and children today. You too may be an overcomer for Christ. For He has offered not only the blessings of victory but the strength to be victorious.

Why not ask Him for this strength now?

Someone at the Door

(Revelation 3:20)

MOTHER! There's someone at the door!"
How often you have said this when you have heard a knock on your front door! And Mother has come hurrying out of the kitchen, patting her hair in place or drying her hands on a towel. Perhaps she has said to you, "Quickly now, put your toys away; tidy things up; it may be the pastor."

Then the visitor has turned out to be the mail carrier or a salesperson or the next-door neighbor, who has come to borrow the lawn mower. A knock on the door is always exciting, for you never can tell who may have come to see you.

Suppose when you opened the door someday, you would see Jesus standing there! That *would* be a surprise, wouldn't it? What would you do? What would you say?

It's not impossible, for in His message to the church in Laodicea, Jesus said, "Here I am! I stand at the door and knock. If anyone hears my voice and opens the door, I will come in and eat with him, and he with me."

176

SOMEONE AT THE DOOR

What a beautiful picture! We see Jesus standing outside the door, gently knocking. Waiting to come in. Eager to come in. Listening for the click of the latch that will tell Him He is welcome.

Of course Jesus was thinking of the door of the heart. He wanted everybody—rich and poor, old and young, parents and children—to know that He wanted to come and live with them always. He longed to make every heart His home.

Jesus had said this very same thing to His disciples sixty years before, and John had written it down. "If anyone loves me, he will obey my teaching. My Father will love him, and we will come to him and make our home with him." *

How very beautiful! If *anyone*—any man, any woman, any boy, any girl—is willing, God will make His home in his heart.

I know it doesn't seem possible, but it must be true, for here Jesus says again, "Here I am! I stand at the door and knock. If *anyone* hears my voice and opens the door, I will come in and eat with him, and he with me."

That "anyone" includes you.

MARCUS MASHBURN

He won't open the door Himself. He's too polite for that. Anyway, the knob is on the inside, and you have to turn it.

Maybe you can hear a knock just now. There's Someone at the door! Someone very lovely, very kind, very dear.

Don't leave Him standing there! Don't keep Him waiting outside while you tidy things up. Fling wide the door in warmest welcome. Say, "Jesus, I'm so glad You've come. Please live in my heart forever!"

* John 14:23.

The Throne of God

(Revelation 4 and 5)

J UST as John was thinking about Jesus standing at the door of his heart, he happened to look up, and there was a door open into heaven.

"Come up here," Jesus said to him, "and I will show you what must take place after this."

John didn't need a second invitation. He was eager to look into heaven and find out what was going to happen in the future. So he peered through that open door, and what wonderful things he saw!

In the center of everything was the throne of God, a sight so glorious that he couldn't find words to describe it. A wonderful light shone from it, and all around it was "a rainbow, resembling an emerald." In front of the throne was what appeared to be "a sea of glass, clear as crystal." Around it were 24 other thrones where the 24 elders sat, "dressed in white" with "crowns of gold on their heads."

Then John noticed four strange creatures he had never seen before. One was like a

180

lion, another like an ox, another had a face like a man, and the fourth looked like a flying eagle. "They were covered with eyes, in front and in back" as if they were watching everything that was going on. And they never stopped singing "Holy, holy, holy is the Lord God Almighty, who was, and is, and is to come."

Now John's attention was drawn to the glorious Being on the throne. In His right hand He held a scroll with writing on it, which was "sealed with seven seals."

This must contain the story of the future that Jesus promised to tell me, he thought. And he was right. But first the scroll had to be opened.

Suddenly an angel called out in a loud voice, "Who is worthy to break the seals and open the scroll?"

There was no answer. It seemed as if the scroll must remain unopened. John wept, he was so disappointed.

Then a voice said to him, "Do not weep! See, the Lion of the tribe of Judah, the Root of David, has triumphed. He is able to open the scroll and its seven seals."

John looked around for a lion and instead "saw a Lamb, looking as if it had been slain." It was a symbol of Jesus, of course, and when He came forward to open the scroll, the 24

elders sang a new song, saying, "You are worthy to take the scroll and to open its seals, because you were slain, and with your blood you purchased men for God from every tribe and language and people and nation. You have made them to be a kingdom and priests to serve our God, and they will reign on the earth."

Then John heard the most wonderful music he had ever listened to. It came from many angels, "thousands upon thousands, and ten thousand times ten thousand" of them. They seemed to fill all heaven, and they were singing heaven's hallelujah chorus, "Worthy is the Lamb, who was slain, to receive power and wealth and wisdom and strength and honor and glory and praise!"

The majestic sound swelled louder and louder until it seemed that every creature in heaven and on earth was joining in this glorious song of triumph: "To him who sits on the throne and to the Lamb be praise and honor and glory and power, for ever and ever!"

Horses of History

(Revelation 6 and 8:1)

W HEN Jesus began to open the seals and unroll the scroll, it was just as if He had switched on a television set. One picture after another passed before John's eyes, each one a symbol of some event to happen in the future.

First he saw "a white horse! Its rider held a bow, and he was given a crown, and he rode out as a conqueror bent on conquest."

John recognized the rider. It was Jesus Himself. The horse was His church, gloriously white in its first love and purity, as it went galloping with the gospel through all the Roman Empire.

As the second seal was opened "another horse came out, a fiery red one. Its rider was given power to take peace from the earth. . . . To him was given a large sword."

John must have wondered what this could possibly mean. When the third seal was opened, he was even more puzzled when he saw "a black horse! Its rider was holding a pair of scales in his hand."

184

But the fourth scene was strangest of all, for this horse was pale. "Its rider was named Death, and Hades was following close behind him. They were given power . . . to kill by sword, famine and plague, and by the wild beasts of the earth."

Whether Jesus explained these scenes to John we are not told, but looking back across the years, we can understand them clearly enough. The four horses were horses of history. They pictured the story of the church of Christ for the next 1,500 years and more.

They showed how the church, once pure and beautiful, would lose its first love and become hardened and quarrelsome, seeking power from the government rather than from God. Then it would forget that the gospel is free to all and would actually sell its blessings for money. And finally it would become the very opposite of all that Jesus intended it to be. Instead of offering life, it would bring death to millions through its cruel persecutions.

It is hard to understand how Jesus could know that all these things would happen long before they did! But He knew. History shows that His church was spoiled by sin just as He said it would be.

If the heavenly TV had stopped at this point, John might have thought that the preaching of the gospel would be a total failure and that Satan would win the long struggle between good and evil after all. But this was not the end of the story.

When the fifth seal was opened, John caught a glimpse of all the faithful followers of Jesus who had been put to death because of their love and loyalty to Him. He heard a voice tell them to "wait a little longer, until the number of their fellow servants and brothers who were to be killed as they had been was completed." God had not forgotten them. They would be rewarded very soon.

Then, when the sixth seal was opened, "there was a great earthquake. The sun turned black like sackcloth made of goat

hair, the whole moon turned blood red, and the stars in the sky fell to earth, as late figs drop from a fig tree when shaken by a strong wind. The sky receded like a scroll, rolling up, and every mountain and island was removed from its place.

"Then the kings of the earth, the princes, the generals, the rich, the mighty, and every slave and every free man hid in caves and among the rocks of the mountains. They called to the mountains and the rocks, 'Fall on us and hide us from the face of him who sits on the throne and from the wrath of the Lamb! For the great day of their wrath has come, and who can stand?'"

What a tremendous scene! Now John knew without a doubt that Christ would keep His promise to return in glory, and when He came, He would deal with all those who had treated His faithful ones so cruelly.

The "great earthquake" may well refer to the one that shook the world in 1755, as the fearful persecutions of the Dark Ages were coming to an end. The darkening of the sun and the bloodlike appearance of the moon took place on May 19, 1780, as we found when we studied Jesus' other prophecy about His second coming in Matthew 24 and Luke 21. The stars fell on the night of November 12-13, 1833, leaving only the final scenes in this picture yet to happen.

What about the seventh seal?

"When he opened the seventh seal, there was silence in heaven for about half an hour."

Silence in heaven? How? Why? Because Jesus and all the angels will have come to this earth for His final triumph. On their return, heaven will ring again with His praise.

If all these scenes suddenly appeared on your television set some evening, how would they affect you? If you saw the four horses galloping through history, picturing the sad, sad story of the church—what would you think? If you saw the promised signs of Christ's return—the great earthquake, the darkened sun, the blood-red moon, the falling stars—what would you say? And if you saw Him riding down the skies in all His glory, what would you do?

It's time to be thinking about these things, for His coming is very near, "right at the door." *

* Matthew 24:33.

God Marks His Own

(Revelation 7:3)

H AVE you ever divided a bag of candy among a group of friends? If so, as you passed the pieces around I suppose you said, "One for *you* and one for *you* and one for *you* and one for *me*." And then what did you do? I will guess that you picked up your pieces and put a mark on each one, so you would know yours from the others.

In the seventh chapter of the book of Revelation, John tells us that God is going to do some marking too. Just before Jesus returns in glory, He will send a mighty angel all around the world to seal the servants of God in their foreheads.

Of course He is not planning to put a mark like a tattoo on anybody's head. That wouldn't mean a thing. But He will do something in the minds and hearts of men and women, boys and girls, that will be seen in the holy joy on their faces and in the goodness of their lives. All who belong to God will know it. And God will know it too.

John did not explain how this sealing will be done, but Paul made it clear to the Ephesians when he said they "were marked in

189

him with a seal, the promised Holy Spirit." [1] This is how God marks His own. Just as the Holy Spirit leads people to be born again, so He brings them step by step into perfect oneness with Him.

Can anyone know when he or she is sealed? The only way to be sure is to give yourself entirely to God, praying for strength day by day to live in full obedience to His will. This means that you have decided to follow God and His way of life forever, and no one could ever persuade you to change your mind. It means that you will keep His commandments, all 10 of them. It means that you will put no other gods above Him; you will never bow down to an idol of any kind; you will never take His name in vain; you will keep His true Sabbath as a holy day; you will honor your father and mother; you will never kill, or commit adultery, or steal, or lie, or covet your neighbor's goods.

In other words, you will love the Lord your God with all your heart and mind and soul and strength, and your neighbor as yourself. Your heart will be filled to overflowing with the love of God.

In the very last days of earth's history, when God searches among all nations for His people, He will look for those who are so full of His love that they have become a perfect reflection of Him. Not only do they "obey God's commandments and remain faithful to Jesus," [2] but their lives have become beautified with love for God and others. God will tell these people, "You are mine! And you, and you, and you!"

"They will be mine," He says, "in the day when I make up my treasured possession." [3]

Will you be among that happy company? Will you let God mark you as one of His own? Will you let Him seal you for His kingdom?

---

[1] Ephesians 1:13.
[2] Revelation 14:12.
[3] Malachi 3:17.

Last Message of Love

(Revelation 14:6-14)

A S JESUS talked with John on the Isle of Patmos, He spoke again and again about His second coming.

When He opened the seven seals, it was to sketch the outline of events in His church until His advent.

When He caused seven angels to blow their trumpets, it was to reveal the story of the conquerors of the Roman Empire until He, the greatest Conqueror of all, would return. Then "the kingdom of the world" would become "the kingdom of our Lord and of his Christ, and he will reign for ever and ever."

When He told John about sending out seven angels with seven terrible plagues, it was to warn the wicked of what would happen to them in the day of judgment.

And when He let John see the three flying angels, it was to help him understand how hard God will try to save people before their last opportunity to return to Him is gone forever.

The first of the three angels that John saw "flying in mid-air" carried "the eternal gospel" to all who live on the earth, "to every nation, tribe, language and people." And he cried with a

loud voice, "Fear God and give him glory, because the hour of his judgment has come. Worship him who made the heavens, the earth, the sea and the springs of water."

The second angel cried, "Fallen! Fallen is Babylon the Great," while the third added this warning, "If anyone worships the beast and his image and receives his mark on the forehead or on the hand, he, too, will drink of the wine of God's fury, which has been poured full strength into the cup of his wrath."

This threefold message is not really new. It is the same gospel of love that God has been bringing to men since Adam first sinned in Eden. It is the *eternal* gospel, changeless as God Himself.

It is an appeal to everyone in every country, every city, and every home, to turn back to God and worship Him as Creator and Redeemer before it is forever too late to repent.

It is a warning to flee from the foolish sins of "Babylon," to avoid all the agencies of Satan such as "the beast and his image," and to avoid its mark like the plague. For Satan marks his followers too, just as God marks His. But Satan's mark is the

opposite of God's. It is seen in pride, greed, selfishness, and disobedience to His commandments.

When the three flying angels complete their work and disappear into the blue of heaven, far in the distance John sees Someone on a white cloud "with a crown of gold on his head and a sharp sickle in his hand." As the cloud comes nearer and nearer, he realizes that the One on it is none other than Jesus Himself, coming back in glory to get His people.

This is why we know that the three warnings of the flying angels are to come to the world just before Christ's second coming. They are messages for us today.

As you learn more about what the three angels have to say, listen carefully and follow their advice well. They may be God's last messages of love to you.

When Jesus Comes

(Revelation 19:5-19)

HOW LONG John was allowed to look into heaven and to see all the wonderful things Jesus wanted to show him, we do not know. It may have been hours. It could have been several days and nights.

Any doubts he may have had about the return of Jesus were gone now. Any fears he had had that the non-Christian world would destroy the newborn church had vanished too. After all, he had seen the future victory of Jesus over all His enemies! He had watched thousands of angels who were on His side, help to bring it about!

Yet there is more for him to see—another scene of splendor and glory to strengthen his faith in the final triumph of his Lord and Master. Suddenly from the throne comes a voice saying, "Praise our God, all you his servants, you who fear him, both small and great!"

In response, the whole vast multitude of heavenly beings, like "the roar of rushing waters and like loud peals of thunder," cry out, "Hallelujah! For our Lord God Almighty

reigns. Let us rejoice and be glad
and give him glory! For the wedding of the Lamb has come."

The wedding of the Lamb! The wedding of Christ to His
redeemed, the uniting of heaven and earth for all eternity!

Now John sees the Bridegroom coming for His bride. What
a beautiful scene it is!

"I saw heaven standing open," he says, "and there before
me was a white horse, whose rider is called Faithful and True.
With justice he judges and makes war. His eyes are like blazing
fire, and on his head are many crowns. He has a name written
on him that no one knows but he himself. He is dressed in a robe
dipped in blood, and his name is the Word of God.

"The armies of heaven were following him, riding on
white horses and dressed in fine linen, white and clean. Out of

his mouth comes a sharp
sword with which to strike
down the nations. 'He will rule
them with an iron scepter.' He treads
the winepress of the fury of the wrath of
God Almighty. On his robe and on his thigh
he has this name written: KING OF KINGS
AND LORD OF LORDS."

John watches spellbound as the noble procession
sweeps in stately majesty down through the skies. Can this be
the same gentle Jesus he once knew and loved in Galilee? he

198

wonders. Can this be the One who meekly let Himself be crucified on Calvary's cross?

Yes, indeed, the very same. Unchanged with the changing years, but now crowned with the glory and honor He deserves.

But a strange thing happens. "The beast and the kings of the earth" prepare to make war with the invading multitude from heaven. It is a foolish effort. They are swept aside, destroyed "by the splendor of his coming." [1]

Does this mean that nobody will be glad to see Jesus when He comes again? Oh, no. It just tells us what will happen to those who hate Him. His bride will be there waiting for Him— eagerly. His faithful followers will look up with joy saying, "Surely this is our God; we trusted in him, and he saved us. This is the Lord, we trusted in him; let us rejoice and be glad in his salvation." [2]

This is the day when all who have died believing in Jesus will be raised from the

dead. Together with the living saints, they "will be caught up . . . to meet the Lord in the air." [3]

And Jesus will smile at them as a bridegroom smiles at his bride, and He will take them home with Him to the "many rooms" [4] He has prepared for them.

What a day of rejoicing that will be! Will you be glad to see Him too?

[1] 2 Thessalonians 2:8.
[2] Isaiah 25:9.
[3] 1 Thessalonians 4:17.
[4] John 14:2.

Good Wins at Last

(Revelation 20:7-21:2)

NOW JOHN looks far into the future. It seems to him that 1,000 years go by. Then suddenly he sees a beautiful city gliding down through the heavens, shimmering like a star.

Something about it reminds him of Jerusalem. But it isn't the old city he knew before the Romans sacked and burned it. No, it is a city more glorious than any he ever saw or dreamed about. Its foundations, walls, and rooftops are all aglow, shining like many colored jewels.

Gently it settles on the earth. Inside are all God's people. They were taken to heaven at Christ's second coming and look radiantly happy.

Now John's attention is called to another amazing scene. Wherever he looks, graves are opening and people are coming out of them. Millions upon millions. He has never seen so many.

Suddenly John understands. This must be the resurrection

of the wicked people that Jesus talked about long ago.

Now John sees a tall, powerful figure moving among the crowds. There is an evil look on his face, the look of one who knows he has been beaten and wants revenge. It is Satan himself, the great enemy of Christ, who has caused all the trouble and sorrow on the earth since the beginning. Now he is urging the wicked to attack the beautiful city.

"Its streets are made of gold, its gates of pearl," he cries. "Let us go up and take it. We have many more people on our side. Let's go! Let's go!"

Stirred with envy, greed, and hatred, the mighty mass moves forward, marching up "across the breadth of the earth" and surrounding "the camp of God's people, the city he loves."

But that is as far as the wicked get. At that moment God steps in.

Says John: "I saw a great white throne. . . . And I saw the dead, great and small, standing before the throne, and books were opened. Another book was opened, which is the book of life. The dead were judged according to what they had done as recorded in the books. The sea gave up the dead that were in it, and death and Hades gave up the dead that were in

them, and each person was judged according to what he had done."

It is the final judgment. And what a scene it is! Everybody who ever lived on the earth is present. All the good people are inside the city and all the bad people are outside. In His wisdom God has brought everybody together at the same time so that all may understand what He has done and what He is going to do. He wants everyone in His whole vast universe to know that His ways are right and good.

As the books of heaven are opened, not only do the wicked discover that God has kept a record of everything they ever said or did, but they see the whole story of sin from its beginning and what God did to meet it and overcome it. Maybe it will be shown on some sort of giant television screen, perhaps against the background of the sky itself.

They will see how sin began, and Satan's part in it. They will see how he brought the spirit of rebellion to this earth, with all its sad results. They will see Christ offering to pay the penalty of sin in order to save the human race from destruction. And they will see Him hanging on the cross, dying, that all who come to Him may live.

As the wicked look and listen they will realize there was nothing more God could have done to help them.

At last, one by one, the books are closed. The record has been read. The story has been told. There is nothing more to say.

As John wonders what will happen next he sees a blaze of light sweep down from heaven as God mercifully brings the great struggle between good and evil to an end. And "fire came down from heaven and devoured them. And the devil, who deceived them, was thrown into the lake of burning sulfur."

Though it has taken a long, long time, good wins at last.

All Things New

(Revelation 21:1-22:17)

WHEN the smoke has cleared away and John is able to see around him again, it seems that everything has changed. Everything.

The earth is different. The sky is different. Everything is so transformed that John says, "I saw a new heaven and a new earth, for the first heaven and the first earth had passed away."

Nothing marred by sin can be seen anywhere. Everything is gloriously beautiful. The whole earth looks as lovely as it did in the beginning, when God created it. God has made it over again. He has restored Eden, just as He promised. He has made everything new. Nothing is left that ever brought harm or sorrow to the human race.

The same wonderful Being who once created the world with such infinite, painstaking care has now remade it with the same skill and thoughtfulness for His children's eternal enjoyment.

Everywhere John looks he sees beauty beyond compare.

Towering mountains are clothed with stately redwoods, hemlocks, cedars, pines, and oaks. Rolling hills are decorated with flowering trees and shrubs. Masses of flowers spread over the grass-covered fields like a vast, many-colored carpet. Buttercups and daisies, poppies and marigolds, bluebells and daffodils, hollyhocks and snapdragons, geraniums and delphiniums, orchids and begonias—all are here again, as lovely as God first made them.

There is "no longer any sea." No more vast oceans separate people from one another. Instead, beautiful island-studded lakes nestle against the hills, and a sparkling, rippling, cascading stream flows from the Holy City.

John says he saw this "river of the water of life, as clear as crystal, flowing from the throne of God . . . down the middle of the great street of the city." From there it flows on to the ends of the earth, refreshing all nature with the life of God.

As for the New Jerusalem, it is so very beautiful that John can hardly find words to describe it. It is so bright that it shines like "a very precious jewel," he says, "like a jasper, clear as crystal." It has "a great, high wall with twelve gates." Yet it isn't like an old-world fortress, for the wall is of jasper and the gates are of pearl, while the rest of the city is "of pure gold, as pure as glass."

John made a special point of describing the foundations, for they are unique. They are not made of concrete, or brick, or heavy logs, but of all sorts of jewels. As the light from the throne shines through them, they flash and sparkle with gorgeous color.

John looks for a temple, but there isn't one. There's no need for one anymore. No more sacrifice for sin will ever be required, for Jesus made the sacrifice "once for all." * So "the Lord God Almighty and the Lamb are its temple."

"The city does not need the sun or the moon to shine on it, for the glory of God gives it light, and the Lamb is its lamp. . . . On no day will its gates ever be shut, for there will be no night there."

What a wonderful home the dear Lord is preparing for those who love Him! And what a happy one! For He is going to live with His people forever. Tenderly, "he will wipe every tear from their eyes," and nobody will ever be sad again. "There will be no more death." No more mourning. No more crying. No more pain. Only purest happiness forever and ever.

There will be no more grumbling. No more quarreling. No more fighting. Only perfect peace through all eternity.

There will be no more unkindness. No more impatience. No more cutting words or cruel deeds. Only loving friendliness always and always.

Would you like to live in this glorious homeland of God's true and faithful children?

You may. You are invited. "The Spirit and the bride say, 'Come!' And let him who hears say, 'Come!' Whoever is thirsty, let him come."

"Come! Come! Come!"

Jesus is calling you. He wants you to share this new earth with Him. It is the last invitation in the Bible; the last in all the wonderful Bible story.

Why not accept it now?

---

* Hebrews 10:10.

INDEXES

Complete List of the 411 Stories

Bible Men and Women

Great Bible Teachings and Character-building Lessons

Books of the Bible

Complete List of the 411 Stories

← PAINTING BY LARS JUSTINEN

Around every human life that trusts His love and obeys the principles of His kingdom the Heavenly Watcher puts His protective arms and keeps him from dangers seen and unseen.

COMPLETE LIST OF THE 411 STORIES

COMPLETE LIST OF THE 411 STORIES

Bible Men and Women
and Where Found in *The Bible Story*

Great Bible Teachings and Character-building Lessons

CHARACTER-BUILDING LESSONS

CHARACTER-BUILDING LESSONS

Books of the Bible
and Where Mentioned in *The Bible Story*